# AT HOME
## WITH THE
# SPIRIT

## Tom O'Hara SJ

PAULIST PRESS
New York and Mahwah, New Jersey

The poem "Phoenix" by D.H. Lawrence is reprinted from *The Complete Poems of D.H. Lawrence,* edited by V. de Sola Pinto & F. W. Roberts, copyright © 1964, 1971 by Angelo Ravagli and C.M. Weekley, Executors of the Estate of Frieda Lawrence Ravagli; used by permission of Viking Penguin, a division of Penguin Books USA, Inc. The adaption of Psalm 105 is reprinted from *Psalms Now* by Leslie Brandt, copyright © 1973 by Concordia Publishing House, St. Louis, Missouri; reprinted by permission.

Published by arrangement with David Lovell Publishing, Brunswick, Victoria, Australia.

Cover design by Moe Berman.

Library of Congress Cataloging-in-Publication Data

O'Hara, Tom, 1932–
   At home with the Spirit: on retreat in daily life/Tom O'Hara.
   p.  cm.
   ISBN 0-8091-3460-8 (pbk.)
   1. Spiritual exercises.  2. Retreats.  3. Ignatius, of Loyola,
Saint, 1491–1556. Exercitia spiritualia.  4. Catholic Church–
Prayer-books and devotions—English.  I. Title.
BX2182.2.O33   1994
248.3—dc20                                                    93-27210
                                                                      CIP

Published by Paulist Press
997 Macarthur Boulevard
Mahwah, New Jersey 07430

Printed and bound in the
United States of America

# The Basic Principle of Ignatian Spirituality

God, who is Love, creates, sustains and redeems us in Christ, all and each one, in order to share with us the fullness of Life, so that we may glorify God

All the rest of creation God gives us to help us attain our goal. So, in all our relationships and our use of every creature, we must not lose sight of that goal.

Therefore we must develop an attitude before every creature and situation of equilibrium and poise. We should have this attitude about health or sickness, wealth or poverty, honour or shame, a long life or a short life, and all other similar alternatives.

Our one desire and our every choice should lead us more to the goal of our creation.

# *Foreword*

In recent years the Spiritual Exercises of Ignatius of Loyola, the founder of the Society of Jesus, have experienced a renaissance in all the English speaking countries. Jesuits and others have rediscovered the powerful impact these Exercises can have on individuals when tailored to the individual's needs and circumstances. Many people have made the Spiritual Exercises individually directed at retreat houses. However, one need not go away to a retreat house to profit from the Exercises. Among the discoveries of recent years has been the realization that Ignatius himself fostered a remarkable variety of ways of making them. One of his "annotations" or remarks to the director of the Exercises, the nineteenth, speaks of a method of making the Exercises while continuing one's ordinary life, a method which has come to be called the "Retreat in Daily Life." With this method a person takes a certain time each day for formal prayer and reflection on the experience of that prayer time. Each week the retreatant meets with a director to talk about the experiences of the past week and to receive guidance for the prayer of the coming week. In this manner a retreatant with the proper dispositions could make the full Exercises of thirty days in the course of twenty-four to thirty weeks. Of course, the method can be adapted in many ways to fit the time schedule of the person making the retreat. Once one has experienced the desire of God to meet his people wherever they can be met, there is no end to the creative ingenuity that might be used to let God fulfill his desire. This method, often called the method of the nineteenth Annotation, has also been adapted for small groups who come together weekly with a director to share their experiences of prayer during the previous week.

In *At Home with the Spirit: On Retreat in Daily Life,* Fr. Tom O'Hara, S.J., of Australia has distilled his experience of many years in directing people through the Spiritual Exercises in various formats. It is remarkably well done, obviously the work of a director with much experience and fine sensitivity to the myriad ways God is present in our lives. It will prove very helpful to retreat directors who want to try out their wings as directors of such retreats in daily life. Individuals will find it helpful for their own daily prayer. However, it will be most helpful to individuals who go through the experience either with an individual director or with a group of people helped by an experienced director.

I am most happy to introduce this fine book to its American audience. Thanks to Father O'Hara for making his wide experience available in such a simple and attractive form.

*William A. Barry, S.J.*

# Introduction

The renewal and *aggiornamento* called for by the Second Vatican Council has been nowhere more evident than in the field of spirituality. The authentic spirit of many of the Church's great spiritual writers and teachers is being continually more studied and recaptured. At the same time, modern spiritual writers, while striving to be faithful to the great men and women of the past, are searching for new forms of presenting their inspiration in a way that is relevant to our own times.

One of the great spiritual classics of the Church is the little book that St Ignatius titled *The Spiritual Exercises*. In composing this work Ignatius himself was very conscious that spirituality can be neither frozen nor crystallised. He therefore incorporated into his text the basic principles of flexibility and adaptation.

In recent years many adaptations of *The Spiritual Exercises* have been written, endeavouring always to express more clearly their relevance to the late twentieth century, and at the same time to incorporate the best of modern studies in scripture, theology and psychology.

*At Home with the Spirit* is an attempt to make the Spiritual Exercises of St Ignatius available to ordinary men and women in the form of a daily program of scripture reading and prayer. As with all adaptations or translations, there is a constant creative tension between faithfulness to the original and communication with people of today. References to Ignatius and the text of the Exercises are kept to a minimum, while striving to be as faithful as possible to the spirit of both the saint and his book.

The text here has been used extensively by parish groups, especially in the diocese of Parramatta, Sydney, Australia. Beyond its immediate purpose as a program for a praying group, the book has another function. It provides a commentary on the Spiritual Exercises and a plan of personal prayer based on them. As such, it can prove most useful to all those who are making or giving retreats.

# Contents

**At Home with the Spirit**
**Part Three**

# AT HOME
## WITH THE
# SPIRIT

### PART ONE

## Week 1
# *Hope*

The focus of this week's prayer is the Lord's promise to do great things for us through out our lives—and especially during these eight weeks.

I pray over and over for the grace of hope, faith, trust.

I keep trying to get in touch with the feelings the Word of God arouses in me.

Use the following texts in the ways suggested on pages 5-7 on prayer.

### Day 1: Ephesians 3:14–21
How can I experience my hidden self? That deepest part of me, where I am made in God's image, where the Holy Spirit dwells as in a temple. Can I sense what it means for that self to grow strong in the Spirit of Christ?

*'God will do infinitely more than I can ask or imagine.'* How do I feel about this promise? Spend time tasting that feeling.

### Day 2: Psalm 63:1–2.
Desire for God. The most basic reality of the human heart. I repeat over and over: *'Oh God, you are my God; for you I long'.*

I sense God as truly personal and intimate. Pause and taste the feeling. Stay with the feeling.

Repeat the phrase.

### Day 3: 1 Peter 1:3–9
A magnificent text of *hope*.

The Father will bring me to the fulness of life. He promises it to me in Christ. The Father will do great things for me during these eight weeks.

Get in touch with your feelings about the Lord's promise.

### Day 4: Luke 11:1–13
Prayer is infallible. All my prayers will be answered.

God is my loving Father. If I ask my Father for bread, could he give me a stone?

The gift of the Holy Spirit is certain every time I pray.

Talk to the Father; give thanks.

### Day 5: Jeremiah 29:11–14
What are God's plans for me?

They are Good News. God guarantees that I will find him.

During these eight weeks I am invited to seek God with all my heart.

Let me look into my heart and sense this generosity, which is God's *gift* to me.

### Day 6: Isaiah 55
*Come! Accept a free gift! Listen! Come to life!*
*You are my chosen one. I make a covenant with you.*

*I love you and forgive you.*
*My word will accomplish its purpose in you.*
*The trees will clap their hands over us.*

Stay with any words of this chapter that move you.

# Prayer

'Taste and see that the Lord is good' (Psalm 34:8).

The most important part of the Retreat at Home is the daily fifteen minutes of prayer.

The most important thing about the time of prayer is not so much what we do during that time. It is that we are *faithful* to spending that time each day in God's presence.

What can I do to spend the time of prayer most fruitfully?

## 1. Prepare

A few hours before I pray, I must decide what I am to pray about.

What grace do I want now?

What Scripture will I use?

Where and at what time will I pray?

## 2. Commence

Once I have begun, I must not let anything interrupt God's time. Commence *slowly* and *gently*.

All prayer is an activation of my Baptism. I

make the sign of my Baptism, the Sign of the Cross, slowly and *thoughtfully*.

Sometimes I may be gripped by a sense of who the Father, Son, or Holy Spirit is. If so, I do not move on, but spend as much time as I can tasting that feeling.

After the Sign of the Cross, commence with this prayer: 'Lord, I believe that I am in your presence. I ask your grace that during this time all that I do may be directed solely to your glory and the coming of your Kingdom.'

## 3. Personal conversation

One of the most important 'definitions' of prayer is that of Thomas à Kempis: 'Prayer is conversation with Jesus'.

We have all learned to pray like this. It can be very good to spend much of the fifteen minutes talking and *listening* to the Lord.

## 4. Use of Scripture

When praying with a Scripture passage, read it through slowly once or twice.

Now take the passage much more slowly. Stop and taste any word or phrase that speaks to you personally, arouses feelings in you. Keep chewing it over, and resist any temptation to move on to anything else. Gain all the nourishment you can from that word or phrase.

Always include some conversation with the Lord (as in 3 above).

Conclude with a 'formal' prayer—a Hail Mary, the Lord's Prayer—or an aspiration such as: 'Heart of Jesus, burning with love for me, inflame my heart with love for you'.

## 5. Reflection
After each time of prayer, it is very important to reflect upon what has happened.

What struck me? What feelings did I experience?

How did I relate to God? Jesus? Holy Spirit? Mary? Joseph? Anyone else? Prayer is always a personal relationship.

Where is the Lord leading me now? In my prayer? In my life?

*Write down* your reflections to bring to a group meeting.

## 6. Throughout the day.
In so far as you can, try to be in touch with the grace of your fifteen minutes of prayer.

*Note*. Though the time suggested for daily prayer is fifteen minutes, in practice many people do more — or they increase the time as the weeks go by. Still, fifteen minutes seems a reasonable demand for busy people.

## Week 2
# *Images of God*

'God is an infinite being.' This is a philosophical statement, using concepts.

'The Father is vitally interested in what I am doing today.' This is a personal statement, using images.

My personal relationship with God resides in and grows through images rather than concepts.

Both Scripture and daily life propose many God-images to us. I try to get in touch with those that appeal most to me.

### God is love: 1 John 4:16

The image of God, constantly proposed throughout the Old Testament, is that of a faithful lover.

God's love has two aspects:

It is the love that initiates everything.

It is constant, enduring.

A typical example is the wording of the shortest psalm, Psalm 117:

*His love is from all eternity,*
*And his faithfulness lasts forever.*

### Day 1

Below are listed eleven images of God with a corresponding text for each.

Today I spend my fifteen minutes reflecting on these images. I list them in the order of their appeal to me. Number each one 1 to 11.

| | | |
|---|---|---|
| ☐ | Healer | Mark 1:40–45. |
| ☐ | Consoler | John 14:26–27. |
| ☐ | Security | Psalm 18:1–6. |
| ☐ | Liberation from fear | Isaiah 43:1–3. |
| ☐ | Saviour | Titus 3:3–7. |
| ☐ | Father | Luke 11:1–13, Ps. 103:13. |
| ☐ | Shepherd | Psalm 23. John 10:11. |
| ☐ | Forgiver | John 8:1–11. |
| ☐ | Giver of all gifts | Psalm 68:9–10. |
| ☐ | God of nature | Psalm 8. Matt. 6:26–30. |
| ☐ | Creator | Genesis 1:26–31. |

## Day 2
Use for prayer the text corresponding to my favourite image.

## Day 3
Use for prayer the text corresponding to my second choice.

## Day 4
Use for prayer the text corresponding to my number 12 choice.

## Day 5
Use for prayer the text corresponding to my number 11 choice.

**Day 6**
Repeat the prayer of Day 2 (my favourite image).

Throughout the time of the Retreat at Home we may often return to the same texts for prayer. Not only would it be wrong to say: 'What's the use? I've done that one', but it can be very valuable to repeat. This is especially true when we suspect there is something more for us in a text that we haven't got out of it yet. In this case feel free to pray with that text on succeeding days without moving on to others that have been suggested.

# Prayer

The thoughts and feelings experienced during prayer are clearly important. There is always the danger of attaching too much importance to my thoughts. I can be tempted to try to control life through my own thoughts.

Prayer is a relationship in which I submit to God. I try to be open to God's thoughts—expressed in his Word.

In any relationship, feelings are more important than thoughts.

In any relationship with God, *deep* feelings like desire, love, trust, hope, faith, gratitude are most important.

These feelings can be very elusive, hard to touch. I need to ask repeatedly to experience them.

Sometimes during my prayer time there may be no thoughts, feelings or images that I can hold on to. On these occasions it can be good simply to read over a passage of Scripture as slowly as I can, and to keep repeating the process.

Or simply keep repeating a word or phrase. Or simply sit in silence in God's presence.

*Be still and know that I am God* (Psalm 46:10).

Such silence highlights the contemplative dimension of all prayer.

All prayer has a dimension of contemplation. By 'contemplation' we mean that contact with God which takes place in the deepest part of the person (usually called the heart). Such contact takes place through faith and love. It is very difficult or impossible to describe. We know in faith when it is happening.

A helpful distinction for understanding prayer can be the following:

*Prayer*: a profound attitude of heart in God's presence (contemplation).

*prayer*: an activity by which we try to cultivate Prayer.


### The Weekly Meeting

The style of meeting that directly fosters our personal relationship with God is a *sharing* meeting. It differs from a discussion meeting.

In *discussion* I express my *thoughts*. An appropriate aspect of discussion is the attempt to persuade others of the truth of my thoughts. There is room for disagreement. A temptation is to try to use power and manipulation, rather than friendly persuasion.

In *sharing* I tell the story of my *experience*.

In order to do this I should write down each day

what struck me during my prayer—the images I found helpful, the feelings I had, the parts of the conversation which moved me, the insights into my life I experienced. When it is my time to speak, I must speak of my experience in the first person singular—simply, directly, trustingly. *Listening* openly, lovingly, attentively will be the main contribution each one of us makes to the life of the group.

In a *sharing* group there is no room for disagreement. There is no need to persuade. There is no manipulation. Rather than directly exercise power, I make myself vulnerable. Sharing evokes response, never disagreement. Such response can be empathy, affirmation, support, a word of thanks. Through the listening and sharing of each, the life of the group grows. As the letter to the Ephesians puts it: *Speaking the truth in love, we grow in all ways into Christ, who is the head ... So the body grows until it has built itself up in love* (4:15–16).

Week 3

# My Personal
# Graced History

To the question 'Who is God?' a Jew would always reply: 'God is the one who ...', and go on to tell the story of God's great deeds for his People. To describe *experiences*. On the other hand, we were taught, when young, to reply in *concepts:* 'God is the creator of the world, the infinite being without beginning and without end'. I need to get in touch with the story of God's deeds in my life. The story of my life up to this moment is a love story, the story of God's constantly communicating himself to me and my response to that communication.

I reflect on the various stages of my life, seeing how all-embracing and constant God's love has been.

For each period of life here are some 'trigger' words and reflections. If any special experience of the Lord's love comes to mind, simply stay with that, sensing gratitude, trust, love.

### Day 1: Psalm 139:13–14. Infancy, the first five years.
I imagine myself beginning from one fertilised ovum in my mother's womb.

God is at work, creating, shaping, forming, loving me.

The love of my parents and family: How they taught me to smile, to experience joy, to love. How they cared for and protected me.

I was made one with Christ in Baptism. I thank God.

### Day 2: Luke 2:39-40. Early school years.
My sense of home, of belonging. The continuing love of my family.

The teachers who gave their best efforts to caring for my development. My young friends. The experience of joy, wonder, love—birthdays, outings, games, holidays.

God at work in my life. My First Communion.

### Day 3: Luke 2:51-52. Adolescent years.
Growth, education, understanding life. New friends, excitement, idealism.

People who have inspired me: teachers, leaders, heroes.

Difficulties overcome, grown through.

The Lord guiding me through rough ways and smooth.

The Sacrament of Confirmation at work in me.

### Day 4: Matthew 3:13-17. Young adulthood.
Gifts of maturity and freedom. New choices. New friends. New love.

The new dimension of family. Marriage? Children?

Behold my servant in whom my soul delights ...
filled with the Holy Spirit and with power.

### Day 5: Luke 4:16-30. The Middle Years.
My successes and failures. Fulfilment. The exercise of power (we all have it!). Leadership.

The rhythm of work and relaxation. God always at work, constant in love through thick and thin.

Praise to the Father, Son and Holy Spirit.


### Day 6: Psalm 105. Recent years.
The Lord working now through my experience of change in Church and society.

Perhaps use for prayer the adaptation of Psalm 105 below (page 16).

# Prayer

The way of praying most practised in our Christian tradition is the re-living in imagination of a gospel mystery. We see it at work in the liturgy, and in sacramentals like the Rosary, the Christmas crib, the Stations of the Cross.

As we use the gospels, let us reflect upon this way of praying. The imagination is extremely important for putting me in touch with reality. All my personal relationships exist in my imagination.

Dreams, visions, expectations, symbols, all the richnesses of personal life reside in my imagination. This is far more real than steel and concrete!

The prayerful use of the imagination puts me in touch with the risen Lord, present in my life here and now. He is the same Lord Jesus who walked the roads of Palestine all those many years ago.

As I pray with the gospel, I try through my imagination to have a sense of presence to what is happening in the gospel story.

I use all my senses: I see, hear, touch, taste, smell.

It may sometimes happen that my imagination 'takes over' and carries me into the story. Perhaps I become one of the persons taking part in the drama. I feel I am really there.

This is not a clear use of my physical senses. The images may be vague and elusive, but they give me a sense of presence.

It sometimes happens too that thoughts, feelings, images 'dry up'. When this happens I simply stay with God's presence, which seems like absence. I am content to 'do nothing'. I 'waste time' with him. I am being truly *contemplative*.

## An Adaptation of Psalm 105
(from *Psalms Now*, by Leslie Brandt)

How great is my God, and how I live to sing his praises!

Whereas I am often frightened when I think about the future, confused and disturbed by the rapidly changing events about me, my heart is secured and made glad when I remember how he has cared for me throughout the past.

When I was brought forth from my mother's womb, God's hand was upon me.

Through parents and people who cared, he loved

and sheltered me, and set me upon his course for my life.

Through illness and accident God has sustained me.

Around pitfalls and precipices he has safely led me.

When I became rebellious and struck out on my own, he waited patiently for me to return.

When I fell on my face in weakness and failure, he gently set me upon my feet again.

He did not always prevent me from hurting myself, but he took me back to heal my wounds.

Even out of the broken pieces of my defeats, he created a vessel of beauty and usefulness.

Through trials and errors, failures and successes, my God has cared for me.

From infancy to adulthood he has never let me go.

His love has led me—or followed me—through the valleys of sorrow and the highlands of joy, through times of want and years of abundance.

He has bridged impassable rivers, and moved impossible mountains.

Sometimes through me, sometimes in spite of me, he seeks to accomplish his purpose in my life.

He has kept me through the stormy past, he will secure and guide me through the perilous future.

I need never be afraid, no matter how uncertain may be the months or years ahead of me.

How great is my God, and how I love to sing his praises.

Read Psalm 105 from your Bible. Perhaps you could write your own personal adaptation of this psalm.

Week 4
# God Loves Me

B oth in the Old and New Testaments the inspired writers speak of God's love, often putting the words of love into his own mouth.

During this week I ponder some of those words. I allow myself the luxury of being loved and of feeling good about it.

I pray often for the grace of experiencing God's love, the grace to allow God to love me.

### Day 1: Isaiah 41:8-16

The Lord speaks not only to his people, Israel, but to each one of us personally.

I dwell on one phrase that touches me.

Perhaps: *'Do not be afraid, for I am with you'* or *'I have chosen you, not rejected you'* or *'I am holding you by the right hand'* or any phrase that especially appeals to me.

### Day 2: Hosea 11:1-4

Can I sense the Father lifting me like a baby and holding me against his cheek?

Perhaps I let my imagination dwell on this, or on God the loving Father guiding me like a toddler in a harness.

### Day 3: Romans 8:35-39

Nothing can separate me from the love of God—absolutely nothing.

It is interesting that the *first* possibility that Paul considers is 'being anxious or troubled'.

Can I allow my anxieties to come to mind, and experience the power of God's love to overcome every one of them?

God's love is made *visible* in Christ. Can I see Christ in my imagination?


### Day 4: 1 John 4:7-19

God *is* love.

God lives in me.

I am made in his image. I am the temple of the Holy Spirit.

I live in God. He is the air I breathe. Can I sense myself breathing in the love of God with every breath I take?


### Day 5: Psalm 103

The psalm uses words that are very powerful in their symbolism of love.

Can I taste the flavour of words like 'God's kindness' ... 'forgiving' ... 'curing' ... 'redeeming' ... 'tenderness' ... 'renewing' ... 'compassionate'?

As tenderly as a father treats his children, so the Lord treats those who revere him.

God's love lasts from eternity to eternity ... his goodness to their children's children.


### Day 6: Isaiah 43:1-7

Dwell on one phrase that touches you. Perhaps:

*'I have called you by your name; you are mine'.* I hear the Father lovingly say my name.

*'You are precious in my eyes.'*

*'You are honoured ... and I love you.'*

*'I have created you for my glory ... I have formed you.'*

# The Love of God

**B**y love I mean not our love for God, but God's love for us. (1 John 4:10).

Perhaps this is the most important lesson to be learnt about the love of God. This love initiates everything at every moment. The only thing I can do of any value is to receive, accept and respond to God's love. Anything else is sin. The sin of Adam and Eve was to try to appropriate to themselves an autonomy they could not possibly have. Sin is an attempt to take away from God the initiative that is his alone.

All prayers, works, acts of charity have value only in so far as they are responses to the Father's love. My role is to allow his love to flow through me back to him, passing through others on the way. It is only *my* love in so far as it is an acceptance of God's love.

Perhaps this circle could be helpful:

This approach shows what we aim for, rather than a more static, vertical 'two-way' sort of image:

The feeling tone of the vertical model is: God loves me, therefore I should love God. Rather, my role is to allow the Father's love to flow to me and through me—by way of those around me—so that I become less and less of an obstacle to that love.

As the love of God is the foundation of the whole life of the human spirit, this prayer of the fourth week is extremely important.

*I cannot begin to be a human person except in so far as I am loved.* The absolutely basic principle of psychology is that love is essential for the growth of a person. A child who is loved develops healthy, positive attitudes to life, a positive sense of self, and is capable of loving others in turn. Similarly, in the spiritual life, the receiving and accepting of God's love enables me to pass that love on to others, and also back to God.

Love belongs to the affections. It transforms the whole person, but it resides primarily in the affections. These affections are deeper than what we usually mean by feelings. Scripture speaks of the love of God with a power that can touch the affections of the heart. It is very appropriate for the feelings to be involved (it feels good to be loved!), but it is not essential. When I am loved and love, I am aware that there is something deeper than feelings happening inside me.

So, the Lord invites me to hear his words of love within, to ponder the words he speaks to his people in Scripture, and to let these words have their effect in my heart. This kind of prayer is called *Affective Prayer*. It is very important to move to this level in my prayer, not to fixate simply on the level of thinking and talking in prayer. It is OK to think and talk, but the affections must also become involved. To experience these affections is a gift. I must ask for it if I am to be ready to receive it.

*An excellent way of preparing myself to receive this gift is to repeat over and over a phrase in which the Lord speaks of his love.* Say the phrase; try to taste the feeling of it; repeat it; taste; repeat it.

All human love is inadequate. It is a pale reflection of the infinite love for which we were created. My life experiences of being inadequately loved can leave me wounded, in need of healing. The experience of divine love is the ultimate healing of every wound; so this kind of affective prayer can be a very powerful means of healing. Every prayer is ultimately the receiving of God's love. Thus one of the most excellent ways of praying is simply to sit in God's presence and allow him to love me. If I let God love me, an authentic response to that love will surely follow.

## Week 5

# Response to God's Love

*'What return will I make to the Lord for all his goodness to me?'* Psalm 116:12

In Scripture there is only one proper attitude in the face of God's infinite, personal love. This is *total* response. I am called to love God with *all* my heart.

Sin is failure to love God with all my love. To respond in love does not mean that all my weakness and sinfulness must suddenly disappear. It means that as the moment of grace comes to me, I must say a simple and total 'yes'.

It is not a matter of 'trying harder'. It is always a matter of experiencing God's love for me and allowing the response of my human heart to come. Refer back to the circle of love on page 21.

### Day 1: Luke 1:26-38

This story recalls to us *the* model of human response.

I use my imagination to be present to Mary.

She is young, small, fragile, living in the 'backwater' village of Nazareth.

She does not jump to a response as soon as the

angel appears. Rather she listens—very long and attentively.

She hears God's words of love: 'You are highly favoured', 'Do not be afraid, Mary', 'The Lord is with you.'

Mary seeks much clarification. It is only when she hears 'Nothing is impossible with God' that she says 'Yes'.

Mary's 'Yes' is primarily passive: 'Let it happen'. It is total.

Let me feel my desire to join in her 'Yes'.

Let me ask again and again for that grace.

### Day 2:
Repeat the above contemplation of the Annunciation to Mary.

### Day 3: Deuteronomy 6:4-7
These words were the prayer of every good Jew every day, and on his/her death-bed. Mary knew this text very well and embraced it totally.

I pray for the same grace according to my gifts. Say these words of Deuteronomy over again and again.

### Day 4: The response of Paul
*For me, to live is Christ* (Philippians 1:21).

*All I want is to know Christ* (Philippians 3:10).

*The love of Christ controls me* (2 Corinthians 5:14).

*In all circumstances I am content* (Philippians 4:11).

*For freedom Christ has set us free* (Galatians 5:1).

## Day 5: Genesis 22:1-18
Abraham's was a total 'Yes' to God, no matter what ... *even if* God should take 'my only hope, my son whom I love with all my heart'.

We must remember, though, that this is an imaginative *story,* a wonderful one, to illustrate the point of total 'Yes' to God. God does not 'play games' with human sacrifice.

## Day 6: Romans 8:18-27
Romans chapter 8 is the most wonderful proclamation of the nature of Christian life. God's own Spirit lives in my heart and can set me free from everything that holds me back. The Spirit empowers me to make a total response.

Speak to God. Give praise. Give thanks.

# The Spiritual Exercises

In 1919 Pope Benedict XV proclaimed St Ignatius of Loyola (founder of the Jesuit order) as patron of all retreats for the universal Church. This proclamation was based on St Ignatius's gift to the Church of his book of the Spiritual Exercises. In this work Ignatius outlines the way of making a retreat of 30 days, an experience designed to have a profound effect on the retreatant's life, making him or her open to a thorough conversion of heart and committed to spending life in

God's service for the coming of the Kingdom, according to a personal call received from God.

Ignatius was born in 1491, converted in 1522, ordained in 1537, founded the Jesuits in 1540, and died in 1556. So he spent as many years, fifteen, giving retreats as a layman as he did as a Jesuit. His spirituality is for all. In the post-Vatican II renewal the Spiritual Exercises have been followed by laity, by priests and by religious of many different spiritual traditions, as well as by members of other faiths.

There are many different ways of adapting the Spiritual Exercises to different types of retreats. The Retreat at Home is one of these. The basis for these adaptations, and for the Retreat at Home is provided by St Ignatius in the book of the Spiritual Exercises.

The Spiritual Exercises provide a very rich, gospel-based spirituality. They are theologically very sound. They are practical and full of psychological insight confirmed by the best of modern psychology. This is why so many people find them relevant to our own times.

The Exercises start with a powerful statement of the total love of God in creating each of us, and the call for total response to that love. This was called by St Ignatius 'The First Principle and Foundation'. It is at the beginning of this book under the title 'Basic Principle of Ignatian Spirituality'.

In making the Spiritual Exercises of 30 days a person would normally spend the first few days pondering the truths of the Basic Principle. This is what we have been doing in the first four weeks of our Retreat at Home. *It can be very helpful at this time to read over often the Basic Principle, so as to become thoroughly familiar with it.* In it Ignatius gives us his inspiring vision of God, creation, and human responsibility and growth.

The remainder of the first week of a 30-day retreat is devoted to opening oneself to the Lord's gift of conversion of heart. This is our program for Weeks 6 to 8 (pages 33-48).

Just as the Basic Principle gives the program for the whole Spiritual Exercises, after the first week Ignatius gives us the program of all the rest in the great meditation of the Call of Christ (often called the 'Kingdom Meditation'). This meditation is the first week of our second Retreat at Home (pages 51-6).

Retreat at Home 2 focuses on response in discipleship to the Lord of the gospels. The constant prayer of this time is to know, love and follow Jesus more. The meditations and contemplations are all geared to listening to the Word in the gospels and applying this to the practicalities of one's own life.

Retreat at Home 3 (pages 101-146) is about the continued following of Christ to and through his Passion and Death to Resurrection. It is a deepening of union with Jesus, to give expression to that union in every aspect and detail of our lives.

In our present Retreat at Home we attend to God's love, healing and total forgiveness, which enable our human and spiritual growth to flourish as fully as possible. The subsequent Retreats at Home will go to deeper levels of freedom from self and union with Christ.

## Process and Content

So far we have been focusing on the *material* of the Spiritual Exercises—what one does. Far more important is what is called the *process*. Each week, as well as the texts for meditation or contemplation, there is a corresponding explanation of the process of the Exercises. Our program gives us the scripture and the spiritual theology involved in this dynamic progress through the Spiritual Exercises. It is left to each individual with his/her director or each group with its facilitator to 'flesh this out' with appropriate reflections, stories, hymns and activities to promote the process outlined in these theological analyses.

## Some fundamentals of Ignatian process

1. For Ignatius God's Kingdom is realised here and now through the integration of the divine and human, of prayer and action. We help promote this integration through reflection. I reflect on my living in order to know what I want from my prayer. I reflect on my prayer in order to see how it inspires and challenges me to live. The readings given in our program should always be used, in the words of Ignatius, 'to reflect upon myself and draw fruit' (Spiritual Exercises, nos. 106-208, 114-116, 122-125, 194). So, there is a never-ending, ever *deepening* cycle: Action/Experience → Reflection → Articulation (in a journal, with a director, in a weekly meeting) → Prayer → Reflection → Articulation → Decision → Action.

2. Another key part of the process is to respect the rhythm of consolation/desolation, through repetition. *Consolation* is an inner movement of my

spirit towards God (e.g. a sense of trust, a feeling of gratitude, a desire to serve, sorrow for sin, concern for the poor, etc.). *Desolation* is a movement of my spirit away from God (e.g. frustration, boredom, doubt, discouragement, mistrust, etc.). Note that a desolation is not a sin; it is equivalent to temptation.

Throughout the program repetition is suggested. It is of critical importance to understand that repetition is not just to be exercised when the program suggests it. Whenever consolation or desolation is noticed repetition must follow. In repetition I do not try to 'cover the material again', but I focus on that inner movement of my spirit and I pray about it: about consolation in order to deepen it; about desolation in order to be freed from it, so that it may be transformed by God's grace into consolation.

3. Another most important aspect of the process is the movement towards *contemplation*. By Baptism I am in union with God, Father, Son and Holy Spirit. Through contemplation I am in touch with this union at progressively greater depth. My union with God is able more and more to shape my inner attitudes and to flow into my life. Contemplation is not some special, esoteric way of praying; it is the heart dimension of all true prayer. It is a profound attitude of heart in God's presence, it is the realisation of what we possess by the gift of faith and baptism. (On this theme see *I Encountered God* by David Stanley SJ, Institute of Jesuit Sources, St Louis, 1986).

## Continuity and Discontinuity

These words touch upon a fundamental philosophical problem about human nature, which underlies many aspects of making a retreat. It is the old problem of 'the Sunday Christian'. How do prayer and life become one? If everything is prayer, why have set times for praying? As our lives become more integrated, we can become more contemplative in our ordinary living situation. Still the need to withdraw for times of prayer remains. The word 'retreat' implies withdrawal. People go away to special 'retreat houses', usually noted for their atmosphere of peace and quiet, which is a great help to prayer. On the other hand, the Retreat at Home has its advantages in terms of helping the integration of prayer and life.

*The whole enterprise is within the realm of divine grace; hence, as Ignatius stresses continually, the importance of the prayer of petition.* None of my reflections should end in my trying to work things out for myself, but should lead me to be in touch with the grace I need and want, and to pray earnestly for it. Such prayer will infallibly be answered (Luke 11:1-13, John 14:13, 15:16, 16:23). So the whole of the retreat becomes a dynamic interaction between the two poles: prayer and life.

One of the greatest contributions of Ignatius to Christian spirituality is his vision of God's Kingdom as present in a tangible way, of the unity of spiritual life and all other aspects of human living, of the unity between contemplation and action. Hence the whole retreat process culminates in the Contemplation to Attain the Love of God (Retreat at Home 3, weeks 4 to 8, pages 69-100), and one is enabled through constant practice of the Awareness Examen (Retreat at Home 3, week 8, pages 144-6) more and more to 'find God in all things', to be in touch with the presence of the risen Lord in every aspect and detail of one's life.

## Week 6
# *Healing*

In the gospels there are more than twenty stories of personal healing. Each one of these underlines some aspects of the way the risen Lord heals *now* at the end of the twentieth century. They direct us to the attitudes we need to bring for our own personal healing: openness, faith, patience, simplicity, confidence, perseverance.

If there is some hurt in my history that I know I should deal with, it could be best to pray each day of this week in one of the ways suggested pages 36-37. If there is nothing special I wish to deal with, take the following texts day by day.

### Day 1: Hosea 6:1–6
That God will come is as certain as the dawn.

It may help simply to repeat *Maranatha. Come Lord Jesus* (Revelation 22:17,20).

The healing may take 'a day or two' before God comes to raise us up ... or many days!

### Day 2: Luke 15:1-7
Jesus will go after me *until* he finds me. He will *never* give up.

All I have to do is to stop running. Stop refusing

to admit my need of him. Be still in prayer. Let him overtake me. Then he puts me on his shoulders: *'Rejoice with me. I have found my sheep'.*

### Day 3: Mark 1:40-45
Notice the urgency of the leper. He comes running to Jesus, because he is his only hope.

The leper's faith: *'If you want to, you can heal me'. 'Of course I want to'.*

I feel Jesus touch me.

### Day 4: John 5:1-8
No time is too long. This man is healed after thirty-eight years!

Hear Jesus ask me that very searching question: Do you want to be healed?

### Day 5: John 11:1-44
The greatest healing of all.

Lord, the one whom you love (that's me!) is sick.

The sickness (mine) will not end in death but in God's glory. God is more glorified because I am wounded and in need of his healing than he would be if I was fine.

*'Did I not tell you that if you believe you will see the glory of God?'*

Martha has just made a great profession of faith, like one who knows her catechism answers. That faith seems to disappear in the practical situation: *'It's too late, Lord. You can't do anything. By now he will smell'.* I must believe that it is never too late. He can raise even parts of me that I thought were dead.

*Unbind him and let him go free.*

## Day 6: Mark 9:14-29

Once again, *faith.*

> *'Lord I believe; help the little faith that I have.'*

This healing can only be brought about by *prayer.*

The boy has to reach the point of 'being like one dead'. The healing process can be very demanding. But then the Lord raises him up.

This is very different from knowing it in my head. It is in the realm of grace and spiritual experience. I must *pray* for the *gift.*

# Inner Healing

The fruit of Weeks 3 and 4 of our home retreat is the certain knowledge that God is love and has walked with me every step of my life journey, and the experience that God loves me personally.

What then of my experience of evil, of feeling anxious, hurt, rejected, unloved? Perhaps the reflection on my life (Week 3) uncovered areas that I found very hard to look at. Every child is born into a world corrupted by original sin and a history of sin. Sooner or later this sinfulness will affect everyone of us, leaving us hurt, rejected, resentful and anxious.

But the overwhelming truth remains that God is love and loves me in every aspect and detail of my life. God wants nothing more than to heal the hurts of each one of us, if we will let him. If one thing is extremely clear from the gospels, it is that Jesus came to bring healing—not a miraculous cure for a few lucky individuals who happened to meet him, but healing for every human person now, today.

I must respond (Week 5), and cooperate with God's love. A most important, fundamental step in this cooperation is the acceptance of God's gift of healing. I must bring together in my inner life the experience of evil and the experience of God's total love.

The essential first step in the healing process is that I openly face my need for healing. This means admitting this need to myself and revealing my need to another by telling the story of my hurts. This latter step begins to remove the very heavy subjective element in my hurts, to make them more objective. They are moved from the depths of my subjectivity to the 'real' world, the world of God's love. The universal experience is that telling the story in itself brings a large measure of healing. I should return to my life story (Week 3) and admit to myself the main hurts that I still suffer from. I must then be open to telling the story ... to another person ... to the group.

In my prayer I allow my hurts to be confronted by God's love. There are many different ways of doing this. Here are three examples:

1. It may be appropriate to revisit in imagination the scenes of my hurts in the Lord's company—perhaps with him holding me by the hand. I stay there in his presence until I experience the healing power of his love.

2. It may help to sit down opposite an empty

chair (that stands for a person involved in a particular hurt), perhaps with a third chair for the Lord. I enter into dialogue about my hurt.

3. It may be a matter of allowing my pain to come to the surface and repeating a text of Scripture like those from Week 4 (God's love for me) that appeals especially to me.

Whatever method I use, I must stay in the Lord's presence until I experience the power of his love *in* my wound. The historical facts don't change, but my inner attitude does. Those incidents no longer make me resentful, self-centred, distressed. They no longer stifle my spirit: now I am more open to God's Spirit. This prayer for healing is in no sense self-centred. It makes me more united with the Lord, for the greater coming of *his* Kingdom. A healing that I experience is not to be thought of as a 'miraculous cure', and it may not be 'once and for all'. My hurts may return, but if they do it will be in a less powerful form, and I can repeat the process of healing prayer. Through this prayer I know as an experienced truth that 'nothing can separate us from the love of God' (Romans 8:35), and that 'the truth will set you free' (John 8:32).

A very important part of this process is the healing of my distorted images of God. My behaviour can be affected by deep feelings about God as a harsh judge, as a Santa Claus, as a 'mad scientist' who plays games with the world, as a trickster who hides himself and his will and teases us to find him. I need to confront any distorted image I have picked up with the true image of God as Father, Lover, Friend, Liberator. It may well be that the hurt is too deep or the story too long to bring to the group. It is necessary then to seek some personal spiritual direction or, perhaps, counselling.

Week 7

# Sin and Forgiveness

Throughout this week I pray for the grace of knowing in my heart that I am a sinner in need of conversion. I pray to cooperate with the free gift of conversion that the Lord offers me.

The best way to do this is to come before Jesus on the cross and pray for the grace of deep sorrow and even tears for my sins. I allow the love that he has shown to touch me. I could repeat every day the words: *'He loved me and he gave himself up for me'* (Galatians 2:20) or *'Greater love no one has than to lay down his life for his friends'* (John 15:13)

It could help to work through the texts that follow.

### Day 1: Luke 18:9-14

All that is needed is the simple acknowledgement of sin: *'Lord, be merciful to me a sinner'.*

The pharisee makes speeches about it; the publican is aware of God's love and his own need.

I am part pharisee, part publican. Lord, move me by your grace towards the publican's prayer.

### Day 2: Luke 15:11-32

The extraordinary love of the father!

Perhaps I need to enter right into the pig-sty so that I may experience my need of the Father's love.

The father cuts off the son's confession. God celebrates my acknowledgement of my need for his love.

There is part of the elder son in me too. I try to control, to manipulate, to make a contract with God. God asks me to move towards a relationship of total love.

### Day 3: Ezekiel 11:14-21
Can I feel the stoniness of my heart?

Can I believe the Lord's promise to give me a *new* heart?

He can if I will just let him.

### Day 4: John 8:1-11
See and experience the tenderness and compassion of Jesus.

He lowers himself to look up at the woman, to make her feel that she is not hounded or condemned.

He doesn't ask for a confession of her guilt.

He loves and forgives: *'Go, and sin no more'*. This is not a strict command but an empowering word.

### Day 5: Mark 10:46-52
The urgency of the blind man.

He makes a scene; he doesn't care who knows.

I cry out with him: *'Jesus, son of David, have pity on me, a sinner'*.

**Day 6: Psalm 51**

*Have mercy on me, O God, in your great mercy.*
*Instil your joy and gladness into me.*
*Put into me a new and constant spirit.*
*Be my saviour again; renew my joy.*

This is the greatest of the psalms of penance. Experience the power of its cry for mercy, and the psalmist's great joy and confidence in God as he acknowledges sin.

# Redemption and conversion

The starting-point in all Christian spirituality is *redemption*, given as a free gift in Christ.

Receiving this gift requires the acknowledgement of my need—the acknowledgement of sin.

We have all suffered from many distorted attitudes about sin and forgiveness.

The story of sin and forgiveness is the story of God's love. The greatest sign of God's love is forgiveness. To know myself as a sinner, in need of forgiveness, is a very great blessing.

The main distortion to be avoided is that of moving towards guilt and remorse. Guilt and remorse are self-centred, destructive, crippling and unredemptive. They move me away from relationship with the Lord to be locked in myself, as happened in the case of Judas. (Note: Words like guilt and remorse do have another, legitimate use in spiritual theology, as in Psalm 51: 'In guilt was I born'; however, they more often refer to the crippling, negative inner states described here).

The second distortion, closely linked to the first, is to view sin as primarily the breaking of a law. I am easily tempted to get locked into this legalistic approach.

The third, linked to the first two, is that I can avoid sin if I try hard enough. The sin of the pharisees was to try to control sin by their own efforts. This led them to deny sin, and put them beyond redemption.

We need to move away from these distortions to reality. The evil spirit constantly tempts us to fall into them. I must recognize the temptation and resist it.

The reality is that God is love. God created me to love him with my whole heart. To refuse to love God is sin. It is the only sin. Breaches of law are a symptom of the breakdown of this love relationship. The relationship of love led the great saints to see themselves the greatest of sinners. It is a matter of depth in the acknowledgement of sin, knowing it in the heart, not just the head.

In Luke 18:12, all that the publican said was: 'Lord, be merciful to me, a sinner'. This enabled him to receive the free gift of salvation. Another great example of conversion is Peter. When the Lord turned and looked at him, he went out and wept. I, too, must pray for the gift of tears for my sins. They can be a sign of true sorrow—a love of Jesus who loves me so much.

All my prayer for sorrow over the next two weeks must be made in the context of God's love. God does not condemn (Romans 8:34). God is love. God *always* forgives and loves me just as I am. God loves me *in* my sin. My sin is the occasion for greater love and greater grace (Romans 5:20).

When I am secure in this conviction of God's total love, I can look right into the worst of sin and evil (even into hell!) to be moved to greater love. I pray for the grace of being ashamed of my poor response to God's love, and am not in danger of slipping over into destructive guilt and self-reproach. I am good. I am loved. I am made in God's image. I have sinned. I am sorry, even heartbroken. So I love God more for his greatest gift, forgiveness (Luke 7:47).

I can never explain sin or work it out in my head. It is a mystery. I can know in my head about lawbreaking. But to know sin means to experience in my heart (at the same time) God's love, my failure to respond, and his forgiveness.

So I must pray for the grace of having my sin revealed to me. I look at the sins of my past. This is neither an exercise of scruples nor a preparation for confession. It is a help to becoming aware of my *sinfulness,* my constant need for God. I must pray to have this sinfulness revealed to me. I ask, too, to be on my guard against the subtle evil 'values' of the world that lead away from God: greed, self-centredness, materialism, consumerism.

My sinfulness will always be with me, but so will God's grace, forgiving me and leading me through a constant process of conversion from my sinfulness to God's love.

## Week 8
# *Deeper Sorrow*

I continue to pray for the gift of acknowledging (owning) my sinfulness, and the gift of accepting the love of the Father poured out in Christ crucified.

It could be best simply to return each day to Galatians 2:20 or John 15:13, and repeat those words in front of a crucifix. *Holding the crucifix* can be a powerful way of entry into the heart.

Or I may like to use the following texts.

### Day 1: Romans 1:18-2:5 and 2 Samuel 12:1-7
I look at sin 'out there' to see how utterly dreadful it is, then reflect on myself to know that I have done (and do) the very thing I disapprove of.

In both cases, in Paul and David, this acknowledgement leads not to guilt and self-reproach but to love and freedom.

### Day 2: Luke 7:36-50
Can I enter into this scene in my imagination?
   What is my role?
   Am I a bystander? ... Simon? ... the woman?
   What does the Lord say to me? I to him?
   Can I forgive myself enough to let me touch him?
   Am I ready to weep?

### Day 3: Daniel 9:1-19

I pray with Daniel to experience the gift of God's forgiveness.

*Make haste, Lord; change my heart now!*

*To the Lord belong mercy and pardon because we have sinned.*

*Listen, Lord! Lord, forgive.*


### Day 4: Luke 16:19-31

Am I more like the rich man or Lazarus?

Secure in God's love I can look right into the end towards which sin is directed.

In the Father's arms, I look right into hell, secure in the knowledge that he could never let me go there. As I look at the horror of it all, I cling to God all the harder. I give thanks to God.


### Day 5: Luke 6:36-38

The Father treats us all with total compassion.

I too can be compassionate to all.

God does not judge. I can be like that too, forgiving to all, condemning nobody.

Is there anybody I tend to judge? Let me try to see the person as wounded and in need of my compassion. Let me pray for the grace to be forgiving.


### Day 6: Romans 6:1-11

Through faith/Baptism all my sin is forgiven.

I am one with the risen Christ.

His power lives in me, continually leading me away from sin to his love.

# Conversion and reconciliation

During the past seven weeks we have prayed and shared about the love of God, the call for my total response, and about God's offer to me now of the grace of renewal and conversion of heart. God, who is love, is always offering this grace. What we have been doing is trying to attend to this love sufficiently to respond to the grace offered.

The main theme of Scripture is that of sin and forgiveness. This is also the main theme of the collects and prayers over the gifts at the Eucharist. 'Almighty and everlasting God, you show your power especially in your mercy and forgiveness ...' Since this grace is absolutely basic, we spend our eighth and final week praying for it again. Really to know God's love is to know myself as a forgiven sinner. Forgiveness is *the* sign of God's love.

In our overemphasis on the legal aspect of sin, we tend to want to 'clean the slate', 'go to confession', have the *feeling* of being ready for a new start. The reason why our new starts are so often unsuccessful is that we have not got to the heart of the matter of sin and reconciliation. We will undergo a true conversion of heart when we have really prayed though sin and forgiveness. I can then really touch and activate the desire in my heart to love the Lord totally. The Sacrament of Reconciliation then becomes a celebration of the Lord's love, a sacramental encounter with the risen Lord. If it is truly like this for me, frequent celebration of this sacrament can be a great help to growth in God's love. In so far as I am still bound up with overemphasis on the 'confession' side of Reconciliation, I need to experience healing (see Week 6). I need to be set free from fear, from guilt, from legalism.

Powerful guilt feelings, remorse, self-rejection are reinforced by a too individualistic approach to sin and forgiveness. There are dimensions of sinfulness we share in belonging to all kinds of groups in society. Quite unwittingly I adopt the sinful attitudes that belong to the Western world, to the consumer society, to the male sex, etc. The communal celebration of Reconciliation can be a great help. It moves the emphasis away from any obsession with *my* guilt to a sense that we are a people that is sinful, forgiven and loved.

Sin (failure to love the Lord with our whole heart) doesn't suddenly disappear from our lives. Our sinfulness always remains. But so does God's love, which is far more powerful. We are in a continuous process of growth, as a people and as individuals, through the endlessly repeated cycle of sin and forgiveness. At the same time it remains true that there are times of real conversion. Great 'leaps forward' do occur. I must enter into the prayer of penance and forgiveness with great expectations that God will bring these about for me.

One of the surest tests that I have responded to the gift of God's forgiveness is my compassion towards all others who, in their sin, are the recipients of the same divine love and mercy as myself. I cannot possibly be like the unjust servant in Mathew 18, who, having been forgiven an enormous debt, throttled his fellow-servant who owed him a small amount. The spirit of criticism and of radical discontent with an imperfect, sinful world disappears from my heart.

Reconciliation is not only of the individual with God, but of a person with all of creation, with all other persons and with the self. God forgives me. That is no problem. The problem lies in my guilt-ridden inability to forgive myself.

The gift of forgiveness is *free*. Yet it can only be received by accepting the Way, which is Christ. Through faith and Baptism I must enter into his life, his way, which is ultimately the way of the cross and resurrection. The reception of the gift of conversion carries with it the inevitable corollary of discipleship.

But that's another story—the story of At Home with the Spirit 2.

# AT HOME
## WITH THE
# SPIRIT

PART TWO

Week 1

# Following Christ

During this week we pray that we may make a loving and generous response to the invitation of Jesus to follow his way.

### Day 1

I pray in gratitude for the gift of forgiveness, a totally free gift given to me by Jesus and costing him Calvary. I come before the crucifix and keep reminding myself over and over again that *'he loved me and delivered himself for me'* (Galatians 2:20).

### Day 2: Romans 8

This is one of the greatest chapters in the whole of Scripture, in which St Paul spells out the gifts given to the Christian through redemption.

The Spirit is poured into my heart, making me God's child.

Where the Spirit of the Lord is, there is freedom, the glorious liberty of the children of God. I am free to love, free to be whatever I want (spiritually). Can I sense this freedom?

## Day 3: How will I use this freedom?

What do I want to be? What do I want to do?

What is my dream? I search my memory for times of inspiration when I was ready to give myself totally. What is my dream *now*?

Whatever form my natural dream takes, underneath it is *the* dream of desiring to be another Christ.

St Ignatius dreamt of serving a great, noble Christian king in a crusade, and found beneath that the dream of serving Christ in the great struggle against evil in the world.

Do I want to join Jesus in the fight against evil?

Do I want to struggle for true justice and peace?

I speak to Jesus about the desires I find in my heart.

I pray for the grace to say 'yes' to his call.


## Day 4

If I have become aware of my desire to live in union with Jesus, to struggle with him against the powerful forces of evil in our world, I now look a little deeper into the mystery of discipleship to see how this is to be carried out.

First, I remind myself that I am called to follow not a vague ideal but a real flesh-and-blood person. About 1960 years ago, Jesus of Nazareth really walked the roads of Palestine. Let me dwell on this in my imagination.

I attend to the words of Jesus: *'The disciple is not above the master'* (Matthew 10:24) and *'My servant must follow me, so that where I am he also may be'* (John 12:26). Really to follow Jesus is to overcome my selfishness and pride, to allow my ego to be deflated, to 'empty myself' as he did (Philippians 2:7). I try to offer myself to follow the Lord in these words, or in words of my own:

'Jesus you are my Lord, and the Lord of all creation. In the presence of Mary your Mother and all the saints, I want to offer myself to your service. With your help, it is my deliberate wish to follow you on the way of generous love and service. I want to be emptied of self. I want to accept fully the struggles, trials and difficulties involved in living my human life to the full, as you did. I desire to accept poverty, failure and rejection as ways of being emptied of self and coming into deeper union with you, and so bringing about the coming of your Kingdom.'


### Days 5 and 6

It could be profitable to repeat the prayer of the previous days, stopping at any point in which I need the Lord's grace.

Or I might like to read some of the great texts about the following of the Lord: Hebrews 12:1-4; Luke 5:1-11; John 1:35-51.


# The Call of Christ

In At Home with the Spirit 1 we prayed to make our own the grace of the first phase of Christian spiritual life. That is, the grace of knowing myself to be loved by God, called into life and healed and forgiven through the death/

resurrection of Jesus Christ. This grace is received through faith and made formal, official and sacramental through Baptism. Faith and Baptism are the two sides of the one coin.

The second Retreat is essentially built on At Home with the Spirit 1. In it we spell out what is implicit in the grace of redemption/conversion, in faith/Baptism. All the grace received in these weeks is dependent on the quality of the grace of forgiveness. So it may be appropriate to return from time to time to the foot of the cross, to kneel there and to remind myself: *He loved me, and he delivered himself for me* (Galatians 2:20).

When Jesus came among us, he lived his humanity to the full. *He emptied himself* (Philippians 2:7), that is he poured himself out in total love. It was this love that brought about his crucifixion. He loved so much that he was done to death. So the crucifixion is the proclamation of the love of Jesus, which is the way to eternal life. To accept forgiveness as a free gift necessarily means accepting the way.

More than that, Jesus proclaims: 'I *am* the Way' (John 14:6). My acceptance of salvation as a free gift (the grace of At Home with the Spirit 1) is the acceptance of Jesus as the Way. He is not a way I am to follow from afar, by a kind of external imitation. He is the living Way into whom my life is incorporated. I am to become *conformed to the image of God's Son* (Romans 8:29). I am transformed by an inner quality of life given to me by my union with Christ. This is what faith/Baptism means. During these eight weeks we are concerned with *activating our Baptism,* not allowing it to remain a dead letter. Christ and I are one. This is the constant proclamation of St Paul. By faith and Baptism we are incorporated into Christ. We have entered the tomb with him. We are dead to sin. He empowers us, in so far as we let him, to live a life free from sin. We have risen with the Lord. We now live a new kind of existence that is really the same as that of the Lord *at the Father's right hand* (Ephesians 2:6). This reality is hidden from our eyes at present, but is absolutely true.

All of this is implied in the word 'discipleship'. A common image of the disciple is one who walks after, follows and is taught by a master. The *Christian* disciple, by contrast, is one who is united to and lives with the *same life* as the Master. We have to make this life an active reality by putting on the mind and heart of Christ, his values, and so show forth our union with him in the practical details of our living.

The three goals of At Home with the Spirit 2 are:

1. Getting in touch with my gratitude to Jesus for the gift of redemption, my desire to live in union with him, and offering to commit myself to his Way.

2. Growing in knowledge and love of Jesus, the Word-made-flesh for our salvation.

3. Exploring the values he proclaims in the gospels and applying them to the practical realities of my life.

In the first of the eight weeks our focus is on the first of these three goals. We are invited to make a great offering of ourselves, like that of Day 4 (page 53). I may experience some resistance to this offering. I have not yet fully attained *the glorious liberty of the children of God.* (Romans 8:21). Be patient. All the prayer of the following weeks is designed to lead me towards greater liberty through contemplating my union with Christ, my Lord. As this freedom grows, I will find that I can return to this offering and make it more and more fully.

Week 2

# The Incarnation
# and Christmas

During this week we contemplate the Word-made-flesh of our salvation. Through this contemplation my union with the risen Lord, to whom I am united by Baptism, grows and becomes more active. It is a quiet, hidden growth in my heart. Here I am not so much attending to a message that the gospel may have for me, as to the person of Jesus. He is his message. Can I rest in his presence and grow in his love?

### Day 1: Incarnation
It may help to start with imagining the Blessed Trinity planning the salvation of humanity.

See in imagination all the vastly different races and people of planet earth—all in need of a saviour.

See Father, Son and Holy Spirit taking compassion on us and deciding that the Word should now be made flesh.

Read Luke 1:26-38. This vast panoramic scene takes its focus, and the plan is fulfilled, in the heart of a young girl in a tiny house in the insignificant village of Nazareth.

I have my part to play in bringing salvation to my world—to the whole world.

All I have to do is, like Mary, accept Jesus in my heart. *'Let it happen to me'.*

Try to remain with Mary in great wonder at the Word made flesh at this moment.

Speak to Mary, to Joseph, to the Father, Son and Holy Spirit.

### Day 2: Luke 2:1-20. This is Christmas day!

Re-read the story slowly. The joy. The wonder. The angels, shepherds, good tidings, great joy. Today is born a *saviour.*

*'Fill your minds with these things'* (Philippians 4:8).

Jesus is born in destitute poverty in order to die on Calvary for my salvation. Go to Bethlehem and take part in the events. Speak to Mary, to Joseph. Nurse the baby. See the animals. Smell the damp straw. Immerse your senses. *Taste and see that the Lord is good* (Psalm 34:8).

### Days 3,4,5,6

It would be a mistake to be looking for new material for prayer. In fact our method is to deepen what has gone before in Days 1 and 2.

This is what St Ignatius calls *'repetition'*. This is a technical term. It does not mean: 'Do it all again'. It means that I return to anything from the previous days that really moved me—positively or negatively.

The positive movement is called *'consolation'*.

The negative movement is called *'desolation'*.

*Examples of positive movement (consolation):* I

begin to feel some joy. Perhaps I had lost touch with joy in my life to some degree. I go back to the joyful feelings and pray to be more joyful in my daily living.

I am caught up in wonder at the Incarnation. I return again and again to contemplate and deepen that wonder.

I have noticed St Joseph in a new kind of way. I spend the next prayer times talking to him about it all.

*Examples of negative movement (desolation):* I am too embarrassed to nurse the baby. I keep praying about this until I am able to do it.

'All the different races on earth'. I am aware of negative feelings towards some. I keep praying about these.

I shy away from the poverty element of Bethlehem. I must return to that and pray to overcome this resistance.

These are just a few examples of endless possibilities. The *repetition* in prayer is *extremely* important. It is to be used in all the weeks that follow.

# Contemplating the Lord Jesus

The style of prayer throughout this second Retreat is what is called 'imaginative contemplation'. Go back to At Home with the Spirit 1, pages 15-16. Read over these words on prayer from time to time till you are really familiar with them. See also the note on contemplation on page 11.

Every time I pray I should start with the steps outlined on pages 5-6. Then I begin to ask for the particular grace I desire. Throughout these weeks it is the grace to know, love and follow Jesus, my Lord.

The 'knowledge' that I am seeking is 'heart knowledge', as in Philippians 3:10. *All I want is to know Christ and the power of his resurrection.* It may not mean knowing more about him, but knowing him better in my heart through an intimate and growing personal relationship. One of the main fruits of At Home with the Spirit 2 is that Jesus may become for me a more real, living person with whom I am constantly in touch, rather than some remote, other-worldly figure. I can also grow in relationship with other persons in the great dramas of our Lord's life: Mary, Joseph, Simeon, the Apostles.

The infancy stories were written by Matthew and Luke in order to communicate to their early Christian readers *who Jesus is.* St John does this in philosophical language in the great prologue of his gospel (John 1:1-18). Matthew and Luke do it through highly pictorial, imaginative stories. These stories have a great power to fire our imagination and all the deeper parts of our inner life, our hearts. The writers inform us that the parents of Jesus were Mary and Joseph, that his conception was virginal, that he was born in Bethlehem and grew up in Nazareth. Apart from this we learn no clear certain historical facts from these stories. We learn something far more precious: that Jesus is from the moment of his conception *God-with-us*

(Matthew 1:23); that he is *saviour* for all peoples (Luke).

Contemplation of the Lord's infancy is extremely important. The relationship with the adult Jesus and the Lord of death/resurrection is built on this foundation. There is an ease and delight typified by the attitude of joy and wonder of children before a Christmas crib. In them we see the senses and the imagination at work in the way we are trying to use them now. There is a simplicity and directness and presence to the person of Jesus, to Mary, to Joseph, the shepherds, angels, to the whole *mystery of our salvation.*

What we are doing here is well summed up in the words of Philippians 4:8:

*Finally, brethren, whatever is true, whatever is honourable, whatever is just, whatever is pure, whatever is lovely, whatever is gracious, if there is any excellence, if there is anything worthy of praise, fill your minds with these things.*

We are well aware how our modern media assault our minds with the opposite.

The writer of the first letter of John, who was too late in history to have actually seen Jesus in the flesh, was able to say:

*Something which has existed since the beginning,*
*that we have heard and we have seen with our*
*    own eyes:*
*that we have watched, and touched with our*
*    hands;*
*the Word who is life—this is our subject.*
*This life was made visible:*

*we saw it, and we are giving our testimony,*
*telling you of the eternal life*
*which was with the Father and has been made*
    *visible to us.*
*What we have seen and heard we are telling you,*
*so that you too may be in union with us,*
*as we are in union*
*with the Father, and with his Son, Jesus Christ.*
*We are writing this to you to make your joy*
    *complete.*

What this writer did is what we are doing now. He used the stories of the Tradition to *contemplate* the Lord in *imagination.* If I can do that, I too can *truly* say: 'I have touched him'.

## Week 3
# *Our Salvation Revealed*

W e continue and conclude the contemplation of the Lord in his infancy, asking all
the time for the grace to know him more
clearly, to love him more dearly and to follow him
more nearly, day by day. These words from the
musical *Godspell* go back via St Ignatius (16th
century) to Richard of Chichester (13th century).

### Day 1: Luke 2:22-38. The Presentation in the Temple.
A great scene for contemplation. It is an event
involving much waiting upon the Lord, such as we
need when we contemplate.

A scene of grandeur: the magnificent temple of
the Lord God.

A scene of simplicity and poverty: Joseph, Mary
and Jesus make the offering of poor people.

Observe the wealthy families going that day to
the temple. How differently are Joseph, Mary and
Jesus treated.

Simeon and Anna have spent their whole lives
waiting on the Lord's promise. They have nothing
else.

*Yahweh is waiting to be gracious to you* (Isaiah
30:18).

*All the promises God made find their 'Yes' in him*
(2 Corinthians 1:20).

Now, Lord, dismiss your servant in peace.

I immerse my senses in the scene with Joseph, Mary, Simeon, Anna.

Speak (and listen!) to each one.

### Day 2: Matthew 2:1-21

The coming of the Magi—the wise men from the East. Salvation has come for all peoples—for us, for me.

See the scene: wise men, the star, camels, the gifts, Kind Herod, Jesus, Mary, Joseph.

I bring my gifts: gold (what I hold most precious), frankincense (a symbol of my priesthood), myrrh (for burial, a symbol of suffering).

Imagine Jesus and his parents fleeing to Egypt. The story illustrates the way God the Father who saved Israel out of Egypt saves his Son Jesus out of Egypt, and so saves each of us out of slavery and lack of true freedom.

### Days 3,4,5,6

Time for *repetition,* as explained on page 58. *'Fill your minds with these things.'*

Here are a few more texts which may help me contemplate the Lord and enter more deeply into the mystery of who he is:

*He is the image of the unseen God* (Colossians 1:15).

*In him all the fullness of the divinity dwells bodily* (Colossians 2:9)

*No one has ever seen God. The only Son, who is*

*closest to the Father's heart, has made him known* (John 1:18)

*'I am the Way, the Truth, and the Life'* (John 14:6).

*'Philip, he who sees me sees the Father'* (John 14:9).

*In him are all the treasures of wisdom and knowledge'* (Colossians 2:3).

*Christ Jesus has become our wisdom from God, our justification, our holiness and our freedom* (1 Corinthians 1:30).

*As for Mary, she treasured all these things and pondered them in her heart* (Luke 2:19).

*He then went down to Nazareth and lived under their authority. His mother stored up all these things in her heart. And Jesus increased in wisdom, in stature and in favour with God and men* (Luke 2:51-52).

I may also like to read the story of Jesus' staying behind in the temple (Luke 2:41-50). Like Mary, I ponder it all in *my* heart.

# Freedom

The fruit of At Home with the Spirit 1 can be expressed in many ways. Perhaps one of the most helpful is in terms of *freedom*. I am created in love by God to live freely in this world, always growing in union with him. Re-read the Basic Principle at the beginning of this book. Because of the Fall (original sin), my freedom is restricted in many ways.

The deepest movement of my spirit is towards God. But there are other spontaneous movements, like pride, covetousness, lust, anger, gluttony, envy and sloth—the seven deadly sins—which tend to move me away from God. These movements are not bad in themselves, but they are *tending* towards evil. I can learn (by a life-long process) to re-direct the energy in them in a Godward direction. Then my *whole* life is moving Godwards.

I will not be entirely free of 'the seven deadlies' until I am six feet underground, but I can co-operate with grace to control them rather than have my attitudes and behaviour controlled by them.

Through original sin my affections are out of order. A deep freedom means a re-direction of my affectivity. Conversion of heart brings a new order into my affective life. The contemplation of Jesus in these weeks of Retreat 2 focuses my affection on him, and so purifies it and sets me more and more free.

The fruit of Retreat 1 is vitally important for making Retreat 2 fruitfully. I need to be forgiven if I am to enter into contemplation. As I accept forgiveness more, I am able to enter into contemplation at deeper and deeper levels. It can be helpful to return from time to time to *He loved me and he delivered himself for me* and to the offering from Week 1 Day 4 (on page 52). One of the principal fruits of Retreat 2 is a *growing* freedom.

Two of the main interior movements that restrict our freedom are fear and guilt. Both are emotions that prevent us from relating to others, lock us in on ourselves, immobilise us. In so far as I let Jesus set me free from fear and guilt, I am enabled to move out of myself in love for him and all others. He liberates me from poor self-image (one of the besetting ills of our age) and 'false humility'. Really to be a disciple means to stand up and be counted in the cause of mercy, justice and truth. Perhaps our faith should turn us more into lions rather than into lambs.

We all need to be set free from pharisaical attitudes: legalism, perfectionism, Pelagianism. By 'legalism' we mean limiting ourselves to the minimum we think the law, the rules, demand. By 'perfectionism' we mean an attitude that is harshly self-critical. Whatever I do is 'not good enough'; nothing lives up to the standards of the harsh critic inside me. Neither I, nor others, nor the government, nor anything else is good enough. By 'Pelagianism' I mean an attitude of trying to save myself by my own efforts. I lose touch with the gentle, drawing, challenging grace of God, and try to achieve my salvation by *my* will-power and *my* control. These attitudes are very subtle, and we all suffer from them, often more than we think we do.

We are learning all the time from contact with Jesus in the mysteries of his life a way that is the opposite of the way of the pharisee. Jesus' way is the way of love, mercy, service, justice, truth. It is a way of simplicity and vulnerability, a radical weakness and lack of control over events, persons and situations. All that the truly free person 'possesses' is the power to respond in love.

These values are proclaimed by Jesus throughout his public life, in his deeds and his words, in his whole personality. They are already a dominant theme of the infancy stories. Jesus, Mary and Joseph live a life of 'radical powerlessness'. They are 'pushed around' by forces outside themselves, and they respond always in love and simplicity.

The essence of *true* freedom is the power to respond in love.

*Where the Spirit of the Lord is, there is freedom.* The more free we are, the more we live in the life of God's Spirit. The fruit of the Spirit is *love, peace, joy, patience, kindness, goodness, gentleness, faithfulness, self control* (Galatians 5:22).

Week 4

# The Crucial Struggle

O ur life experience—and the Scriptures—
teach us constantly that our human world
is involved in a great, universal struggle
for supremacy between good and evil. We want
now directly to face this reality. We are not going
to philosophise about it but to get in touch with our
experience of it. In this great war, the battle-line
passes right through the centre of every human
heart. How does it involve *me*?

Our style of prayer this week is 'meditation'
rather than the 'contemplation' of the past two
weeks.

We pray for the grace to understand what is
going on in the world, what is going on in our
heart, and the courage to commit ourselves more
fully to the values of Christ.

### Day 1

St Ignatius presents a great meditation on the two
leaders and their strategies.

We look today at Satan and his way.

The imagination may be a help. Picture Satan
sitting on a high throne of fire and smoke (eye-
catching but insubstantial). He calls his demons to

him and sends them out to every person on earth—including *me*—to entice all into his camp.

The tactics that these evil spirits are to use are:

First: Get people to want more and more possessions.

Second: Lead them on to want to be greatly esteemed and honoured.

Third: Lead them, in consequence, to want to be in total control of their own and other people's existence. This is *pride*, and leads to every other vice.

I pray for the grace to understand how these tactics are at work right through our society.

I pray especially for the grace to understand ways in which Satan tries to lead me away from Christ, and for the grace to resist.

## Day 2

I now look at the way of Jesus, which (point by point) is the exact opposite of the above.

I may use my imagination again. I see Jesus standing before me: his feet on the ground (which is what the word 'humble' literally means). He is simple, straightforward, very attractive. Jesus calls disciples and sends them out over the whole world to lead people in his way. That way is precisely the opposite of the way of evil.

First: Invite people to a simplicity of life-style, so that their hearts are not captivated by possessions.

Second: Help them to accept willingly those things that deflate their ego ... being marginalised, passed over, rejected ... the humiliations that lead to being emptied of self.

Third: Lead them, in consequence, to radical 'self-emptying'. This is *humility,* which leads to every other virtue.

I pray for the grace to understand and appreciate this way of Christ, fulfilled in the lives of good people everywhere. I pray especially for the grace to know how Jesus is inviting me to belong more to his way, to put on his values and attitudes.

I pray, for the courage to say 'yes'.

## Day 3

I go back over the meditations on Day 1 and 2. This is not 'theory'. I keep praying to be realistic, practical about the way I am living and the way Jesus is inviting me to live and to grow.

Remember, it is OK to have and want material possessions, to use all my God-given talents to come to a personal fulfilment and to be esteemed and honoured as a good person. But the evil spirit uses these good tendencies, distorting them and making me lose my way. His temptations are *subtle*.

It is unpleasant to be poor, to be rejected and humiliated. Nobody likes it. But I know in my heart that it is the way to humility and love, so I accept and want it.

We'd all love to be humble without the humiliations. But there is no other way to humility.

## Day 4

Let me take up again the meditations of the previous days. What I am facing here is the very heart of the mystery of good and evil, in order to give myself more whole-heartedly to the following of

71

Christ. He invites me to help him make his Kingdom come (Week 1). This is the way.

The fundamental strategies of good and evil as Ignatius analysed them are clear; and it is clear how they are at work in the lives of people, both the good and the bad.

I must see how these strategies are adapted to me.

My basic temptation may not be to want to be wealthy, honoured and influential, but for every person the same pattern is in operation. The 'riches' that I am tempted to cling to can be *anything* that is not God. Even love of family can be distorted. I must love in the Lord, not possessively but with a 'light grasp'. This does not mean to love less; it means to love more truly and more fully. Perversely, the 'possessions' I cling to can be things like *my* hurts, *my* poor self-image, *my* spirit of criticism, even *my* lack of material possessions!

To be truly poor in spirit is to be open to life, open to God. It is a gift. I must pray for it.

### Days 5 and 6

Let me go back in *repetition* (as explained on page 58).

It may help to ask myself questions like:

• What are the 'riches' that tend to come between me and my God?

• In what ways in my life am I put in touch with my human poverty?

• How can I accept more fruitfully these aspects of my life?

72

I pray earnestly to be wholehearted in following Christ's way:

• I speak to Mary about it (and listen to her). Conclude with a Hail Mary.

• I speak to Jesus about it (and listen). Conclude with an aspiration, such as: 'Sacred Heart of Jesus, I place my trust in you'.

• Speak to the Father about it (and listen). End with the Lord's Prayer.

Throughout the rest of this Retreat, every time I pray about the following of Christ of the gospels, I should repeat this threefold dialogue with Mary, with Jesus, with God the Father—praying for the grace to commit myself wholeheartedly to the way of life of Christ.

# Two Sets of Values

Our daily prayer this week is based on a great meditation to which St Ignatius gave the title 'Two Standards', i.e. the banners of two armies, that of evil (Satan) and that of good (Jesus). It is no use saying: 'I don't like warfare imagery'. The bombs are falling all around us! That is a fact. We are simply invited to face the reality. This image of warfare is at the heart of the gospel message:

*'Every kingdom divided against itself will fall'* (Mathew 12:25).

*'He who is not with me is against me'* (Matthew 12:30).

I meditate upon the Two Standards—but not in order to choose between the two! It is obvious where our choice lies. I meditate in order to make it more clear, and to embrace the values of Christ with a more undivided heart.

The strategy of the evil spirit is adapted to the personality and the weaknesses of each individual. Yet there is always a common thread. I may not see myself as tempted to become a multi-millionaire, gaining prestige, status, power and influence over the destiny of others. But the basic pattern remains. We are all tempted to want to possess and control. To be fully human, however, is to be a *creature*—not to have ultimate control. It is not by chance that the writer of the Adam and Eve story was inspired to see the basic temptation as 'to be like gods': to escape from creaturehood, to have absolute power and control over one's own destiny—over events, over other persons, over life. This is the temptation of the Mr Big of the drug world. It is also the temptation of Mr J. Citizen who uses his wits to outsmart and manipulate his wife or his child, his neighbours or his colleagues. It is refusal to be open to the other. It is withholding of love. Love makes me vulnerable. Vulnerability feels unpleasant. As I am tempted to look after number one and at the expense of those I am called to love.

The structures of our society (business, politics, the media, education, etc.) are all ambivalent. Often they seem to operate out of the strategy of the evil spirit. Yet there are plenty of good people in each field trying to promote genuine values. The presence of the contrary 'values' is abundantly evident. Materialism, consumerism, permissiveness, lack of discipline, sexual irresponsibility (Galatians 5:19), manipulation, dishonesty, the quick and slick, the impressive and insubstantial, the thinly veiled lie, refusal to hear 'the cry of the poor'—we are all conscious of ways all of these permeate every social institution. This being so, none of us can be entirely free from their influence. Hence the importance of this week of prayer for every one of us.

The values of our Lord, Jesus, will be the focus of our prayer over the next five weeks. He came to establish a Kingdom—of mercy, justice and truth. The means of bringing this about are love and service. Love and service require (on the personal level) self-emptying, humility, painstaking effort, discipline, perseverance, simplicity, straightforwardness. There is a place, too, for the use of such talents such as attractiveness, influence for good over people, cleverness, organisation, promotion. But none of these values will help the coming of the Kingdom, except in so far as they are grounded in, and firmly wedded to, Christ's set of values.

The relational values of love and service require in us the personal value of poverty of spirit. To be poor in spirit is to be authentically human, to live as a creature, radically dependent on God and others, open to grow, change and adapt to life in all its dimensions. To be a Christian is to embrace gladly one's poverty of spirit.

Jesus gave us an absolutely clear model of living in poverty of spirit. He was truly free. He was not as ascetical as John the Baptist. He didn't live as a 'desert monk', but mixed with all people. He was equally at home at the rich man's banquet and embracing the outcast leper.

Each of us must give expression to the *essential* poverty of spirit according to our own personal call from God. The outcast, Benedict Joseph Labre, and the Lord Chancellor, Thomas More, are equally saints of poverty of spirit. Whatever my personal call, I cannot be truly poor in spirit without facing squarely and honestly the need for a certain simplicity of lifestyle. The spirit of evil will present all kinds of subtle temptations to the contrary. Each one of us must resist them and face the issue with a deliberate desire to want to live the way of Jesus as fully as possible.

## Week 5
# *Jesus Speaks to Me*

I n the next four weeks we continue to contemplate Jesus, our Lord, in the gospels, asking every day to know, love and follow him.

We may simply rest in his presence, as in Weeks 1 to 3. But there is an added dimension here, the message Jesus has for each one, not only in his person but also in his spoken words:

What is he saying to me?

What is he calling me to?

It can be very helpful to return from time to time to make the great offering of Week 1 Day 4 (see pages 52-3).

*Important*: Every time I pray I must finish (as on page 73) by speaking to Mary, to Jesus and to the Father about my desire, and asking for the grace to follow Jesus totally—in response to his personal call to me.


### Day 1: Matthew 3:13-17
Jesus leaves Mary and goes to the Jordan to be baptized.

See the parting. Even the perfect family life of Nazareth must be sacrificed in answer to the Father's call.

The Baptism is the anointing of Jesus with the

Spirit and the proclamation of his mission. He is to be 'the suffering servant' of Isaiah. Read Isaiah 42:1-9. The Father's word at the Baptism (and Transfiguration) is the opening of this first poem of the suffering servant, calling to mind all the following ones, right up to the great Good Friday one of Isaiah 52-53.

### Day 2: Matthew 4:1-11
These are the radical temptations of our humanness.

Adam, who was man, was tempted to be like a god.

Jesus, who is God, rejects the temptation to act as God.

The great meditation of Week 4 is clearly based on this gospel text. The three temptations are to possessions, honours and pride.

Jesus's response is poverty, acceptance of failure, self-emptying.

### Day 3: Luke 4:16-13
Today we have a very good scene for contemplating: *All eyes were fixed on him ... They were amazed at the gracious words that came from his lips.*

I want to see him, to hear him, to be present to him.

Jesus has initial success, but there soon follows massive rejection. Read Isaiah 61:1-11, the text that Jesus reads in this scene.

How am I called to bring Good News to the poor?

**Days 4,5,6**

I return in repetition (as explained earlier) to anything that moved me positively or negatively on Days 1 to 3.

Repetition is taking up prayer 'where the action is' for each one of us. It will vary from person to person.

*It was essential that Jesus should become completely like his brothers and sisters, so that he could be a compassionate high priest of God's religion, able to atone for human sins. That is, because he has himself been through every temptation, he is able to help others who are tempted* (Hebrews 2:17-18).

*We do not have a high priest incapable of feeling our weaknesses with us; but we have one who has been tempted in every way as we are, though he is without sin* (Hebrews 4:15).

# Happy Are You Poor

One of the strangest anomalies of Christianity is that Christians are thoroughly familiar with the Ten Commandments (with varying numeration) as presented in Exodus 20 and Deuteronomy 5, yet do not know the Beatitudes (Matthew 5, Luke 6). As Christians, most of us make very good Jews!

The reason for the anomaly is perhaps pedagogical. Law is clearly enunciated, formalised, structured, but spirit is elusive, difficult to grasp, rather like the wind (John 3:8). We are not so comfortable with what cannot be 'pinned down' or 'learnt off'. We begin by learning the Commandments, and in many cases fail to advance to the Beatitudes. As St Paul insists, the Law was our guardian or tutor (read carefully Galatians 3:23 - 4:7) until the time when the Spirit was given to set us free and take us to a new way of life beyond the Law.

Matthew wrote his gospel for Jews, to teach them that Jesus brought about the fulfilment of the Law and the Prophets. He has a constant refrain: *In order that the Scripture might be fulfilled.*

The foundation of the Old Covenant was Moses' going up the mountain to receive from God the Decalogue—a term that literally means 'the Ten Words' of God. Correspondingly, for Matthew the foundation of the New Covenant is Jesus going up the mountain (Matthew 5) and proclaiming eight new life-giving Words of God, the Beatitudes. Luke does not have Matthew's preoccupation about the fulfilment of the Law, so for him the humble, down-to-earth Jesus presents the Beatitudes standing on a plain (Luke 6). Luke gives four Beatitudes. There is no magic in the numbers: ten, eight, four. It is the Spirit that gives life.

Jesus comes *not to abolish the Law, but to bring it to fulfilment.* (Matthew 5:17). His teaching goes beyond the Law. It is *radically* new. It is life-giving. The Law does not give life. During Retreat 2 we are endeavouring to 'put on the mind of Christ', to be disciples, to live according to the spirit of the Beatitudes. We cannot live the letter of the Beatitudes as we can the letter of the Law, precisely because the Beatitudes are about *spirit*.

Perhaps it is not necessary to learn them by heart, but it doesn't do any harm!

The Beatitudes do not come in the form 'Thou shalt/Thou shalt not', but 'Happy are those who'. Jesus is proclaiming that living in touch with the true and deep desires of our heart produces a wonderful, profound happiness. All of his teaching is about the *fundamental nature* of human life. It is not some 'optional extra' for a marginal sect called 'Christians'. The Beatitudes proclaim the fundamental values of authentic, human existence. They go below the superficial to a profound wisdom of the heart. On the surface, poverty, hunger, thirst, meekness, persecution, rejection seem to be the opposite of happiness. Jesus teaches that in embracing willingly these aspects of our human life, true happiness can be found. There is a radical paradox at the heart of human existence. The Beatitudes empower us not to escape that paradox but to celebrate it.

The title of this section is the first beatitude of Luke. Jesus looks directly and with great compassion at the poor people standing around him and says to them, 'Happy are you poor'. Matthew rather enunciates a universal principle: 'Happy are the poor in spirit'. There is nothing good about poverty in itself, except that it can save us from some of the temptations of the rich. It is the inner attitude of heart, the acceptance, that brings happiness. Material poverty has no spiritual value apart from poverty of spirit. The evil spirit will use a sentence like the previous one to tempt us: 'Well then, go for poverty of spirit, without the actual poverty; have your cake and eat it. Be humble, but avoid humiliation'. I must pray throughout Retreat 2 to be *genuine* in my following of the way of Jesus in joyful poverty of spirit, and also in joyful material poverty, if and when he calls me to that. It is guaranteed that I *will* receive such a call, at least at the moment of death.

The only way to put on the attitudes that are 'the mind of Christ' is through love. Hence the importance of the contemplations, gazing long and lovingly at him as I follow his life through reading the gospels.

## Week 6
# *The Way of the Lord*

W e look at scenes in which Jesus is proclaiming the radical gospel values, and
addressing them to each of us in a different, personal way.

I ask to know, love and follow him more, and I
pray for the grace to make real decisions for my life
based on his word to me.

### Day 1: Matthew 5:1-16
Go up to the mountain. Join in the picnic on the
grassy slope.

Be present. See Jesus. Hear him. Ask to love
him.

Ponder each of the Beatitudes. These are the
way to deep, true happiness. They correspond to
the desires of my heart.

### Day 2: Luke 5:1-11
Once again, be present at the scene. I am there in
whatever way my imagination leads me ... in the
crowd ... in the boat ... speaking to the Lord ...
hearing his invitation.

*'Put out into the deep'*: the basic invitation of
faith. Leave the familiar and comfortable. Respond

to challenge. Be really involved with people who don't appeal to me.

*'Leave me, Lord; I am a sinner.'* But, like Peter, I cling to him as I say these words.

### Day 3: Mark 10:17-31
*Jesus looked at him and loved him.*

I open myself up to that gaze. I return the look.

Because Jesus loved him, he invited the young man to give up everything. The young man couldn't accept the challenge. He went away sad. There is only one way to true happiness—to let nothing come between me and the Lord.

What are the 'possessions' I cling to? Write them down.

### Day 4: Matthew 6:25-34
Once again, in these Days 4, 5 and 6, the best thing to do is *repetition.* I pray about whatever has touched me personally on Days 1, 2 and 3.

To be Christian is to be called to put my trust in the Providence of a loving Father.

I would love to be as free as the birds of the air.

The way is to ask myself: do I put my trust in anything else that is not God?

### Day 5: Philippians 3:3-16
Nothing has any value compared with my relationship with the Lord Jesus.

*For his sake I have suffered the loss of everything*—because for my sake Jesus certainly suffered the loss of everything.

**Day 6: Matthew 13:44-46**

Always the same message.

Today we contemplate the beautiful images of the pearl and the treasure. They require the sacrifice of *everything* else.

The invitation to the sacrifice comes lovingly from the lips of Jesus himself.

# The Broken Image

I'd like to pursue the thought that the poor, the ignorant, the sick and the lonely have much to teach us about our own poverty.

*Poverty* reaches right to the depths of each of us; it often touches hidden fears and anxieties, provokes prejudices and even anger. Poverty, as lived by the destitute, the derelict, the alcoholic, the drug addict, and above all the lonely and isolated, challenges the very values of our own living. It unleashes forces within us that we are hard pressed to understand, until we begin to recognize and strip away the hidden but well-established non-gospel values in our lives.

*Destitution* does not mean simply being without money or assets; it means living without power, without a voice in decisions made about one's own life. Because the poor are at the mercy of those with power and authority, they are essentially powerless. Dereliction shows itself as living with little sense of care for self or family or friends, as living without a sense of responsibility. Derelicts belong to no one, belong nowhere. Moreover, if they are alcoholic, they are caught in a never-ending illness. They are 'bound down'.

Although this poverty of destitution is descriptive of the actual living conditions of only a small percentage of our community, their essential condition of being without power, without belonging, and living 'bound down' is real in the lives of each of us. Those who belong nowhere challenge the quality of our own belonging.

When we stand before the derelict and humbly look him or her full in the face, we begin to change. The frightening thing for us is that we can succumb so easily to the pleasure of power. We seek to control, to dominate, to manipulate, to have things our own way. The powerless one reminds us that in so far as we are consumed with power we fail to call that person forth to be part of our lives in Jesus, our brother.

*Homelessness* confronts us just as much as dereliction and destitution. The homeless are often accused of having walked away from the responsibilities of life, especially those of family and work. They seek a place of refuge where opting out is accepted without censure. Confronted with the reality of the homeless, it is for us to make sense of what they mean for our life. Vulnerable as the circumstances of their lives make the homeless, each has a history of hidden reasons, which we will never know, and never have the right to know.

*Non-belonging:* Irrespective of how or why, those who are homeless, derelict, destitute, impoverished human beings belong nowhere, and yet they have that same yearning as all of us to belong somewhere. The key to understanding such people's homelessness is not their irresponsibility, or filth, or anger; it's their *non-belonging.*

For many reasons the homeless belongs to no family, no place, no community, no society: they belong nowhere. And they put us on edge because we claim we belong in all sorts of ways: in a family, a marriage, a church, a shelter, a religious house or convent. What then of the quality of our belonging? How many of us are 'derelict in spirit' within our marriages, our families, our communities, our friendships? And what of that social manner of belonging that breeds status and privilege? While we lay claim to the equality of all, we still tend to believe that some are slightly more equal than others.

The poor and the broken invite us to be part of their lives, and so share in the way that was expressed and lived out by Jesus, the God who became homeless for our sake. It is vital that we approach not with a sense of our own strength, but respectfully, and with a profound sense of our own brokenness.

Obviously it is necessary that help be organised for the homeless and broken on an institutional level, to meet basic needs, such as food, shelter and clothing; however, that presumes and builds on the prior, direct and personal meeting with the broken one. There is a danger of operating only at the 'hand-out' level, where we are in effect one step removed from the reality of the broken ones. We never quite manage to come first-hand into their presence; we keep safe. This keeps us from being confronted and challenged on the personal level of our own brokenness.

I lay no claim at all to having the right approach

to those who are broken; rather I feel a need to speak to the reflective experience of my own mistakes and my own sinfulness. For I too am broken and in need of understanding and care.

(Excerpts from an article by Brother Alex McDonald SJ)

## Week 7
# *Stepping out in Faith*

**F**aith is a personal relationship with our Lord, Jesus Christ.

A personal relationship can only grow and flourish by a sharing of life. We are invited in At Home in the Spirit 2 to grow in faith, which necessarily implies living more fully according to the values that Jesus proclaims—both in his words and in the way that he lives and loves.

### Day 1: John 6:1-15
Another picnic. I go in imagination, and participate in the scene and the events.

This chapter is Eucharistic: in fact it is John's only presentation of the Eucharist:

*He took bread, said the blessing, broke the bread and gave it to them.* These are the central elements of the Eucharist that we re-enact each time we celebrate.

The little boy hands over everything he has and for this reason, though so small, it becomes the food that feeds so many.

### Day 2: Matthew 14:22-23
A great and famous scene!

A wonderful image of faith: leaving my boat in

response to the invitation of Jesus; getting out into the insecurity of water, waves and strong winds.

We can do this if, and only if, we keep our eyes fixed on Jesus. We cry to him:

'Lord, save me; I perish.'

*There was a headwind*—it is always so in our Christian lives. We always need to hear the word of the Lord: *'Courage! It is I. Do not be afraid'.*

### Day 3: Matthew 16:13-20 and John 6:67-71

The great profession of faith of Peter, expressed in two different forms.

I hear the Lord searchingly ask me the question:

*'Who do you say that I am?'*

*'Will you also walk away?'*

What is my faith? Not what others have told me about Jesus. Who is the Lord in my life? What has the Father in heaven revealed to me in my life about his Son?

### Day 4: Galatians 5

Always bear in mind the importance of *repetition*.

This chapter of Galatians is one of the great presentations of the two ways: that of 'the flesh' (i.e. the unredeemed person, or the way of 'this world') as opposed to the way of the Spirit.

We each experience both sets of movements. Let us pray for the gift of discernment in order to embrace those that lead to the fruit of the Spirit: love, peace, joy, patience, kindness, goodness, gentleness, faithfulness, self-control.

### Day 5: 1 Corinthians 1 and 2
It is only the acceptance of the cross of Christ that opens us to his Spirit, and so enables us to judge rightly.

With the Spirit we judge rightly the value of everything.

### Day 6: Romans 8
In this chapter we have the great description of Christian life.

The freedom the Spirit brings. Adoptive sonship. A new way of praying. A new intimacy with the Father. Total confidence.

# Discernment of Spirits

Both in making major decisions based on faith and in the daily living of our Christian lives, discernment of spirits is of capital importance. Every Christian does it more or less consciously. One of the fruits of Retreat 2 is to make us more aware of our lives as disciples, and so more skilled in discernment. Here we can only touch upon this important, extensive subject. A good and detailed treatment can be found in *Weeds Among the Wheat* by Thomas Green SJ.

Absolutely basic to discernment is the kind of freedom (from self) that is the fruit of At Home with the Spirit 1, and which is described to some extent in Week 3 (see pages 65-8). Discernment is very closely linked to the great meditation of the Crucial Struggle and the Two Sets of Values of

Week 4 (pages 69-76). Both the good spirit and the evil spirit are continually at work in the human heart. This is no cause for distress. It is the reality of our humanness. We must calmly accept our human condition (we will never in this life be entirely free of the movements towards evil) and give our attention to identifying these movements, in order to embrace willingly those that lead us to the building of the Lord's Kingdom.

The practice of discernment enables a person to enjoy a certain inner space, not to be *tossed one way and another and carried along by every wind* (Ephesians 4:14). As we grow in discernment, we are progressively more able to stand back from our own spontaneous, subjective movements and make truly free, creative, human decisions.

In the following lists are some of the movements more characteristic of the good spirit and the evil spirit that we all experience. Discernment involves being in touch with and judging these movements.

| The Evil Spirit | The Good Spirit |
|---|---|
| Locked into my own expectations. | Open to growth and development. |
| Closure. Quick to judge. | Openness. Remaining in process. |
| Impatience. | Time is not the enemy. |
| Arrival. | Journey, pilgrimage |
| Be perfect ... | Grow ... |
| By my own efforts. Pelagianism. | In Response. All is gift. |
| Control. | Poverty of spirit. Vulnerability. |

| | |
|---|---|
| Grabbing. Compulsion. Anxiety. | Light grasp. Freedom. |
| Rigidity. | Flexibility. |
| Fear. | Confidence. |
| Guilt. | Sorrow. |
| Moralising. Endless 'shoulds'. | In touch with real desires. |
| *Denial* (of these movements!) | *Acceptance* (of humanness). |
| Self-rejection. | Self-worth. |
| Violence to oneself. | Gentleness. |
| Competitiveness. | Self-acceptance. |
| Exaggeration ... 'No-one ever tells me anything'. | Moderation. Balance. |
| Doubt. Self-doubt. | Self-assertion. |
| Distortion. Illusion. | Truth. Reality. |
| Self-centred: 'I ... I ... I ...' | In relationship ... with the Lord. |
| Subtleties. | Clarity. |
| Moodiness. | I am more than my moods. |
| Turmoil. | Peace. |
| Darkness. | Light. |
| Depression. | Cry for help. |
| Discouragement. | Encouragement. |
| Despair. | Hope. |

These lists must not be regarded as a series of

'bad' words on the left, and 'good' words on the right. The words can be indicators of different spirits or influences at work. A spiritual or discerning person is one who is able to notice these different influences and freely to choose to move with the ones that are leading towards God.

A movement towards evil is no cause for consternation or panic. It is allowed by God. If we identify it properly and deal with it, the movement is transformed. The energy in the movement is re-directed into a movement for good. This is clearly true of the 'seven deadlies' (see page 66), all of which could be included in the left-handed column above. There is no sin in feeling angry, lustful, jealous,etc. Sin only comes in a *free* decision to consent to such a movement. The movements clearly 'energise' us, wake us up from any lethargy we might be experiencing. We can make use of this energy to pray or to act in a constructive way.

## Week 8
# *Jesus Gives All*

Over the past seven weeks we have been contemplating Jesus and listening to the proclamation of his message. His way is the way of love, service, truthfulness and openness to poverty, failure and rejection. He totally 'pours himself out', 'empties himself' for others—for us, for the coming of the Kingdom.

Both symbolically and actually this way of the Lord leads to death (and Resurrection). A Christian, like Christ, is called freely to give up his or her life to enter definitively into eternal life.

### Day 1: Mark 9:1-12
The Transfiguration—a great scene to contemplate, in which to immerse my senses.

Very early in the ministry of Jesus his coming passion, death and resurrection come into sharp focus.

This scene occurs in chapter nine of Mark and Luke (a gospel of twenty-four chapters!). In Luke Jesus deliberately sets out on the road for Jerusalem (9:51).

As the Baptism was the anointing of Jesus with the Spirit for his public mission, so now the Transfiguration is a repetition of that anointing for his suffering and death.

There are many elements in this scene associated with the passion. Principally, Jesus is again proclaimed by the voice from heaven as the suffering servant (Isaiah 42:1).

### Day 2: Mark 8:31-38 and 9:30-37
From the time of the Transfiguration, Jesus speaks often of his coming death. Each time he insists that being a disciple involves following him all the way.

The apostles always fail to understand. So do we. This message runs contrary to our instinct for self-preservation. It is spiritual. It can only be heard through grace. It belongs to contemplation rather than reason.

The paradox: *'Anyone who tries to save his life will lose it; anyone who loses his life for my sake will find it.'* This is the only saying of Jesus to appear in all four gospels. In all, it appears six times.

'What does it profit a person?': we recall the great saying of Ignatius to Francis Xavier.

Immediately after his great profession of faith, Peter has to hear to words: *'Get behind me, Satan'!*

### Day 3: Mark 10:32-45
The contrast between the way of genuine discipleship and the 'human' desire to be the greatest.

It is only through a gift of grace that I can accept the 'hard' sayings of Jesus. See Matthew 20 for the role of Mrs Zebedee in this scene.

### Day 4: Matthew 18:1-10 and 11:25-30

Another expression of the condition of discipleship—to be open, trusting, vulnerable as a little child.

### Day 5:Philippians 2:1-11

Love, community, unselfishness involve having the attitude of Jesus. Paul gives us the greatest hymn to Christ and his total giving of himself. Jesus emptied himself. He became obedient to death.

### Day 6: John 12:20-28

John combines three elements of preparation for the Passion: the sayings about discipleship (notice especially the 'grain of wheat' which appears only here); part of the Gethsemane prayer; and the Transfiguration (the voice from heaven). Jesus' ministry appears to fail: see John 12:37.

# Decision for Christ

J esus call each of us by name into his way, according to our personal gifts and talents. We are free to respond. The more we come into union with him through contemplation, and so through love, the more free we are. Response involves decision.

Over the past eight weeks we have been growing in faith (personal relationship with Jesus) and in love. We have been hearing the gospel values that are the basis of our decisions. We are now *more* free to respond.

Decision itself is a very profound, liberating, human experience. The temptations not to decide are always strong. We are tempted to continue 'muddling along'. Temptations come in the form of putting a decision on the long finger: our intentions remain in the realm of velleities, pious intentions—'I'd love to ... but ...'. Or sometimes we wriggle and squirm over a decision, looking for ways out, being ready to promise anything except the one difficult thing that we know we must face up to. We must pray for the *grace* to be generous and honest in responding to the personal call of Christ.

It is important that I make truly practical decisions that will help the Kingdom to come effectively in my life and my world. Such decisions have two characteristics:

—They grow out of the deep interior life of the spirit.
—They are truly realistic and practical.

It may well be that I am called to struggle with some decision that has not yet fully matured, and the appropriate response is to continue in the prayer and to struggle to apply the values that we have been considering. Don't fall into the 'long finger' temptation!

Every one of us is called to:

—a personal relationship with Christ
—to help make his Kingdom come
—through love and service
—to the poverty, humility and emptiness of self that free us for love.

Re-read and pray over the great offering that is

found on page 53.

I must look at all aspects of my life in the light of gospel values.

Some of the following words may trigger questions that I should consider:

*The persons in my life:* Family, extended family, friends, neighbours, enemies. Parish. Ecumenism. The poor, minority groups, The handicapped, public life, the 'world community'. The old, the next generation.

*Justice:* At home, at work, to the broader community. My social and political responsibilities. Anything I can do? Sharing my possessions. To whom/what do I contribute? Any adjustments needed? With whom am I personally involved? What is my response to persons of the Third World? What projects/organisations do I support?

*Spiritual life:* Prayer, frequency of sacraments, reading. The media: what do I watch? read? listen to? How do I counteract anti-Christian values?

*Holistic health:* Balance of work, interpersonal life, relaxation, play. Healthy attitudes to food and drink, use of drugs (legal ones!)

*Write down what a decision for Christ means at this time of my life.* Living this decision for Christ will involve my sharing in his suffering and death, and in so far as I share that, sharing also his risen life. Contemplation of the Lord's Passion and his Life of Glory is a very powerful *confirmation* of a decision made for Christ. They *strengthen* me quietly to live out that decision with commitment.

The contemplation of the Lord in his Paschal Mystery is the scope of At Home with the Spirit 3, which completes the process of deeper entry into relationship with God in Christ.

# AT HOME
## WITH THE
# SPIRIT

PART THREE

# Jesus Prepares for Death and Resurrection

The gospels of Mark and Matthew lead us through the early ministry of Jesus to a climax—Peter's great confession of faith (Mark 8; Matthew 16). Immediately, the focus shifts to his coming death/resurrection.

Luke especially emphasises Jesus' 'passing in Jerusalem' (Luke 9:31). The rest of his gospel is dominated by the sentence: *He set his face to go to Jerusalem* (Luke 9:51).

### Day 1: Philippians 3:3-16, with focus on 3:10

*All I want is to know Christ and the power of his resurrection, and to share in his sufferings, that I too may attain the resurrection.*

Notice carefully the order: resurrection, death, resurrection.

Suffering is never for its own sake but in view of resurrection—the hope of which precedes suffering, the achievement of which follows suffering.

Can I want resurrection so much that I also want to share in the Lord's suffering?

## Day 2: 'Anyone who loses his life for my sake will find it' (Mark 8:35)

*'A grain of wheat must die to bear fruit'* (John 12:24).

The first of these is the only saying of Jesus to appear in all four gospels. In all it appears six times. It is the essence of the gospel.

I reflect on my experience of human life to see how these verses are the basic law of all life.

I pray earnestly to accept this great mystery of life.

## Day 3: Mark 8:31-38; 9:30-37; 10:32-45

Jesus openly faces the mystery of life/death, for himself and for his followers. Every time the disciples react with an argument about who is the greatest. It is only through prayer that I can move from their attitude to that of Jesus.

## Day 4: Transfiguration. Luke 9:28-36

At the Transfiguration the Father proclaims Jesus as his beloved Son and as Suffering Servant. This is a repetition of the Baptism proclamation.

Just as Jesus was anointed for his public ministry, so now he is anointed for his death/resurrection.

This transfigured glimpse of glory comes before the suffering and death to strengthen the disciples—and us.

The disciples are overcome with confusion at the awesome symbolism: cloud, shadow, brightness, men long dead, proclamation of suffering.

Can I enter into the awe of this mystery?

### Day 5: Luke 22:19-20

Even at this moment in Luke's gospel, the disciples are arguing about who will be the greatest.

*'This is my body given for you ... my blood poured out for you.'*

We lovingly contemplate Jesus accepting his coming suffering and giving himself for us in the Eucharist.

### Day 6: Repetition

There is far more in these mysteries than a person can absorb in one week.

*Always* respect the principle of repetition, i.e. leaving the material aside to remain in the Lord's presence with anything that is moving me towards him—or with any struggle that I am having in totally accepting him.

# In Union with the Lord

The subject for our contemplation in At Home with the Spirit 3 is the suffering, death and resurrection of our Lord, Jesus Christ. We do not approach this sequence simply to complete the story of his life, but to follow through the inner dynamism of the spiritual life. We are loved by God, healed and forgiven (Retreat 1). So, we are called to follow the Way, who is Jesus (Retreat 2). A very important aspect of response to that call is a personal decision to shape my life according to gospel values (final part of Retreat 2).

Any living by gospel values will involve the surrender of my self-centred life to live in union with Christ crucified, and so to live in union with him in his risen Life. At Home in the Spirit 3 can be a very powerful means of confirming a decision made in Retreat 2, and of obtaining the grace of commitment to living out such a decision.

Quite apart from any such practical decision, Retreat 3 situates a person clearly in the perspective of all Christian living. No matter what may be the particular movement of my present interior life, it is fostered and the appropriate graces are obtained through contemplating the Lord in his paschal mystery. To be a Christian and to live the practical details of Christian life, both entail the way of sacrificial suffering transformed into spiritual joy. The sign of the glorified cross and the Man on it holds primacy of place in all Christian symbolism. This is the way of our Baptism. It is what we celebrate in the Eucharist. It is the Paschal Mystery. So, profound contemplation of the Lord's suffering, death and resurrection enriches both our sacramental life and the living of our daily lives.

We come to Retreat 3 enriched by the grace and practice of prayer of the first two Retreats at Home. The more I have obtained the specific fruits of these two, the more deeply I can be drawn into the present contemplation. In so far as my relationship with Jesus has grown through contemplating him in the gospels, I will be more moved by his passion, and so more ready to share in the Spirit he pours out in his resurrection. Each person has spent much time in prayer in the previous two retreats. It is impossible to do this without moving to deeper levels of contemplation. This is important, because the style of prayer in this third retreat is by its nature very contemplative.

By contemplation we do not mean necessarily quiet time, unruffled, free from distraction. Contemplation takes place on the very interior, almost inexpressible, level of union with the Lord. It is quite compatible with struggle and with superficial disturbance. In it he and I are one. So I relive in my life the pattern of his sufferings in order that I may relive the resurrection. In my prayer I enter as fully as possible into both these aspects: the suffering and the joy.

### The grace I pray for

I pray for a growing compassion with Christ in his sufferings, for a deeper sorrow for sin—and for the gift of *tears*.

By its derivation, 'compassion' means 'suffering with'. So I must be open in my prayer to difficulty and struggle if this is what the Lord sends me despite my best efforts. My compassion may take the form of a feeling of warmth towards the Lord, but this is not the only form of 'suffering-with'. Dryness, inability to concentrate and distraction are simple, unpleasant, very real ways of compassion. As always, the criterion is *'By their fruits you will know them'*. I am receiving this grace if my attitude to the suffering members of Christ in the community around me is becoming more compassionate.

In At Home with the Spirit 1 there was a great emphasis on praying before Jesus on the cross. Here is that emphasis again; but with a difference. In the first retreat the perspective was of Jesus suffering to bring me healing and forgiveness. There was a focus on my need of him, and on the events of my life that needed to be brought for healing and forgiveness. Hopefully I have grown in union with the Lord in discipleship through Retreat 2. Now I am more in the position of being *with* Jesus for others. As a result, there may not be many reflections, many references to myself during this prayer. I may have to be content simply to 'be there'.

Week 2
# Thy Will Be Done

Gethsemane is the key to the whole of the Lord's passion. The essence of the passion is the loving acceptance of the Father's hidden plan of death/resurrection. In Gethsemane we have the resolution of the inner struggle of Jesus to accept. All the rest is the acting out of what Jesus has come to in Gethsemane.

### Day 1: Mark 14:26 and 14:32-42
Notice the context of Mark's account (verse 26). Jesus goes to Gethsemane conscious that he is the Shepherd and the sheep will be scattered.

His mission will fail. The disciples' sleep confirms this. So he is 'deeply distressed and troubled'—very strong words. He was *stumbling* on the ground, so great was his distress.

Stay with Jesus praying in the darkness (both literal and interior). He struggles to hand himself over to the Father in total trust—not just in dying, but in going to his death and failing to keep his community together. The Kingdom has not come.

### Day 2: Matthew 26:30 and 26:36-46
Matthew modifies Mark's words describing Jesus' stress.

He began to grieve. He prostrated himself. Jesus, the Lord, is more in control.

Matthew gives us the three stages of the prayer of Jesus:

1. *'Let this cup pass, nevertheless, thy will be done.'*
2. *'If this cup cannot pass, thy will be done.'*
3. (Implicitly): *'Thy will be done.'*

Enter into the gradual, very profound change brought about in Jesus through his dialogue with the Father and his acceptance of his disciples' weakness in continually falling asleep. He passes from initial distress to serene peace and control.

### Day 3: Luke 22:39-46

Perhaps the very pictorial elements of verses 43-44 help us more easily to enter the scene—the struggle (agony), the sweat like great drops of blood, the angel. These elements seem to have been added by a later scribe to Luke's account which focuses on prayer.

Jesus had the *custom* of praying. Here the central verse is *He knelt down and prayed.*

The prayer of Jesus is framed by the double advice to the disciples: *'Watch and pray that you enter not into temptation'.*

The passion, for Luke, is *the hour of the powers of darkness.*

Each of us is involved in that same crucial struggle.

### Day 4: Hebrew 5:7-10

This is a direct reference to the Gethsemane prayer.

*He learned to obey in the school of suffering.* 'To

obey' literally means 'to hear at depth'.

Jesus was always obedient to the Father, but now he faces a new situation. In truly human fashion he must suffer his way through the experience to hear what the Father is saying now. What the Father says in effect is: 'Trust me'.

Jesus replies: *'Thy will be done'*.


### Day 5: John 12-27 and John 17

John breaks up the Gethsemane prayer into these two parts.

The first involves the struggle of Jesus.

The second (chapter 17) focuses on the implicit content of *'Thy will be done'*. Actually the dominant theme of John 17 is *'Glorify thy name'* ('Hallowed be thy name').


### Day 6

*Repetition,* or take the Lord's Prayer, which is the dominant theme of each of the above Gethsemane accounts.

There is really only one Christian prayer.


# A Love Story

In contemplating the Lord's passion there is a delicate balance to be preserved. The contemplation is always in the context of, and with a view to, the resurrection. What the Father willed for Jesus was that he should be the Lord of all creation. His suffering and death is the necessary, inevitable way to that Lordship. Losing sight of this perspective could lead us up dead-ends of sentimentality, wallowing in suffering, or yielding to our human tendency to sadomasochism.

The key to appreciating the Lord's passion is love. To lose touch with that love would render a consideration of suffering at least meaningless, at worst harmful.

The contemplation of the love involved must always begin from the absolute source of all love: God the Father. The passion all takes place because of the Father's love for Jesus. He loves him enough to will him to be Lord. Perhaps the great love of the Father can be brought home to us by considering how he must, as it were, stand aside with his hands tied and allow Jesus, the one loved totally, to go through all of this. Suffering, which is essentially interior, is often greatest on the part of the one who must stand aside and watch the beloved's more external suffering.

As I contemplate the passion, it can help greatly to start each time by looking at it from the Father's perspective and praying to begin to appreciate God's infinite love.

The second great love to be aware of is the response of Jesus' love for the Father. During this time the Father keeps himself hidden. Jesus must commit everything into his hands and go forward into the darkness in total trust. He enters Gethsemane facing a new and 'absurd' experience that he must go to his death without seeing the Kingdom come. The answer to his prayer involves him in total trust. There is no tangible or visible sign that the whole enterprise is not a failure. Right up to the moment of death, he must trust a Father who seems to have forsaken him. To be open to the Father's love means not only being open to life in all its dimensions, but accepting death while failing to accomplish the most important assignment ever entrusted to any human being. Jesus is always totally open to his Father, but his love for the Father is shown most especially through his suffering and death.

Besides the love of Jesus for the Father, we contemplate the love of Jesus for each of the persons involved: his mother, Peter, Judas, his persecutors, Pilate, Barabbas, the penitent thief—and each person mentioned. We are aware of his love for each person living today, and especially his love for me. *He loved me and he delivered himself for me. Greater love no one has than to lay down his life for his friends.*

Always staying well-grounded in this contemplation of love, we contemplate the sufferings of Jesus. Suffering is primarily interior. Jesus suffers interiorly. First there is the Gethsemane struggle to accept that he must go to his death with no sign that the fragile community of believers will survive. Jesus suffers failure, not in any subjective sense of self-pity ('I'm a failure'), but objectively, horrendously, in the seeming failure of his mission. He who is Justice and Innocence is condemned by perverted human courts in the name of justice. He suffers rejection by his own people, by those he has come to save—even by some of his closest friends. There is the absurdity of it all—an aspect of suffering we often find the most difficult to grapple with. Finally, he must suffer all this alone.

So we come to the physical sufferings of our Lord. These are always to be contemplated in the light of love and of his interior sufferings. The sufferings of violence, scourging, crowning, nailing, death by crucifixion are clearly depicted for us in the gospels. An earlier tradition of preaching used to spell these out in every gruesome detail. Simply observe the Lord's sufferings with the conviction that the greater the suffering and the greater the acceptance with which it is undergone, the greater the love.

## Week 3
# *Jesus on Trial*

During this week I may simply take up one of the four gospel accounts of the passion and read a little each day, pausing wherever I am drawn into contemplation.

Or I may prefer to use the Scripture more eclectically, focusing on the more 'powerful' events.

### Day 1: The Arrest of Jesus. Matthew 26:47-56
The kiss of Judas.

Jesus' first experience of physical violence, which dominates the rest of his life on earth.

The irony of the guards arming 'to the teeth' to arrest him.

His total peace (as a result of the Gethsemane prayer) and acceptance.

### Day 2: Jesus on trial before the Sanhedrin. Matthew 26:57-68
I could focus on the heinous injustice ... the total powerlessness of Jesus ... his silence ... the mockery ... the self-righteousness of Caiaphas.

The 'power' of the closed group. The utter distortion of truth involved in this. The absurdity of the perjured evidence.

Here is the paradigm of all the unjust trials that

have taken place throughout history, that take place on various levels in our own society. I acknowledge my own part in such injustice.

## Day 3: Peter's denials. Luke 22:54-62 and Mark 14:16-72

I let myself be drawn into this powerful drama.

Peter's love for the Lord; his desire to follow him, to be near him. His self-confidence, brashness: *'Even though all these others lose faith, I will not'.*

His utter weakness, caving in even before the maid servant. Totally out of control, he swears that he does not know the man!

*The Lord, turning, looked at Peter. Peter went out and wept bitterly.*

## Day 4: Jesus and Pilate. John 18:28-38 and John 19:6-16

The love of Jesus for Pilate.

His willingness to break the silence of his passion to enter into dialogue with Pilate, who is 'redeemable'. The 'almost' conversion of Pilate.

He has a lot to lose. It is always the same question: 'Am I willing to accept this suffering Lord, who is Truth, no matter what the cost?'

Let me stay with this question.

## Day 5: Jesus and Barabbas. Matthew 27:15-26

Never lose sight of the paramount importance of repetition.

Or, if drawn to it, I may take up this scene.

Bar-abbas is a name meaning 'son of his father'.

So clearly he is intended as a type of every man and woman.

The guilty person is set free, while the all-innocent is condemned. *He loved me and he delivered himself for me.*

### Day 6: The scourging and crowning with thorns. John 19:1-6

Dwell upon these very familiar scenes.

Picture the famous scene often depicted in art as Ecce Homo, where Jesus stands before the crowd silent and bleeding and crowned with thorns as Pilate declares: 'Behold the man'. He is the type of every one of his suffering brothers and sisters.

# Contemplation and Compassion

Contemplation is union. The particular grace of the contemplation of the passion is to be deeply in union with the Lord and the strength to live out that union. It is an openness to the suffering dimension of life. There is no rationale that can 'explain' or 'lessen' suffering and the problem of evil. There is simply a wisdom of the heart, based on love of a person, which enables us to accept suffering in union with Jesus, and, as he did, in loving response to the loving but often hidden will of the Father.

Contemplation of the passion may not lead us into many reflections and insights. In fact, all we may be able to do is to 'be there'; and even staying for the time we have alloted can often be a very great struggle. We want to be with the Lord in his sufferings.

This does not mean that we necessarily experience emotions of pity or sympathy. It is like attending a funeral. We want to be there with our grieving friend. At the same time we may be unable to enter into the depth of grief of our friend who was much closer to the person who died. Far from feeling compassion, we may be aware of feelings of awkwardness and remoteness. Yet we stay. It is the only place for us to be. 'Strangely' our friend is greatly supported and comforted by our presence.

Similarly we contemplate the Lord in his suffering not for any feelings we would like to have, but because it is the only place for us to be.

Jean Laplace SJ accurately describes what has been the experience of countless Christians as they contemplate the passion:

### The Difficulty: The Wall
'Often at this moment of the retreat, the retreatant runs into disconcerting difficulties—distraction, dryness, inability to concentrate, objections, rationalisations, temptations, the impression that he is wasting his time. On the other hand, he catches a glimpse of the riches hidden in this prayer. He does not want to abandon it, yet he wants something different. He is like a man who powerlessly and unfeelingly witnesses a scene of horror.

'Perhaps, if you experience a similar uneasiness, you are on the way towards reaping the fruit of your prayer ... The reason you are suffering is that you love so little and so poorly that you stand before a wall which hides the mystery from you, a wall you cannot tear down. This suffering, as a matter of fact, places us in our real situation before Christ ... We find ourselves before the real difficulty of prayer. The difficulty of the wall is the invisible barrier, beyond which we shall not cross unless and when God calls us ...

'What we are feeling here will not disappear, for it is the prayer itself. It is a real purgatory, where a man struggles with God in order to be grasped and transformed by him.

'The passion makes us remain before this wall, until one day, God makes the obstacle fall; and the joy of his presence will then console us for our many years of helpless waiting.

'We experience this difficulty especially when confronted with the passion, and this for two reasons. First because of the object of the prayer. This prayer does not allow us many references to ourselves, unlike the prayer of preceding days. It is a more unselfish prayer, since the Lord occupies, or ought to occupy, the complete field of consciousness. Yet is is also a more austere prayer: it is so delicate that the least distracting breath spoils it. Faced with this prayer, we must agree to be truly poor.

'In fact, these mysteries are only revealed though being lived. They are part of the adventure of faith which we never finish living, as long as we are on this earth. Christ invested his whole life in going towards his passion and "freely entering" into it. We have no means for understanding the passion of Christ other than to continue it in our own life and death. Everything will be explained when everything is consummated. Not before.'

(From Jean Laplace SJ, *An Experience of Life in the Spirit,* Spectrum Publications, 1977, pp.158-159.)

## Week 4
# *Calvary*

W<sup>e</sup> continue to pray for the two graces. Firstly of compassion, i.e. union with Jesus in his suffering, and hence compassion with his suffering members. And secondly deeper sorrow for sin.

Some may find that the best way for them to pray is to hold the crucifix—in silence or while speaking to Jesus on the cross. Others may find it more helpful simply to stand with Mary in her grief each day. Others may prefer to use the Scripture texts that follow.

### Day 1: Luke 23:32-34
Jesus is stripped and nailed.

Enter into the images of these tenth and eleventh Stations of the Cross.

*'Father forgive them ...'* the first of the 'seven last words'.

Contemplate especially the love, the compassion.

### Day 2: Luke 23:35-43
Another of the 'seven last words'.

Contemplate the inner suffering of Jesus at the

mockery and insults, especially from the religious leaders of his own people.

*'This day you will be with me in paradise.'*

Total forgiveness. An absolutely free gift. He does this also for each one of us—for me.

## Day 3: John 19:25-27

Perhaps the best way into contemplation of what Calvary really is, is to enter into the heart of Mary.

To be one with her in love for her Son, in her compassion and grief.

Each of us is welcome here—not because of what we have to offer, but because we are forgiven. Like Mary Magdalen who stands with Mary, I too am a forgiven sinner through the love of Jesus crucified.

## Day 4: The remaining four 'last words'.

*'I thirst'* (John 19:28).

*'My God, my God, why have you forsaken me?'* (Mark 15:34) This is the opening of Psalm 22; perhaps Mark is suggesting that Jesus prays this psalm.

*'Father, into your hands I commend my spirit'* (Luke 23:46).

*'It is consummated'* (John 19:30).

## Day 5: Good Friday. Jesus dies

## Day 6: Holy Saturday. Mark 15:42-47

*They closed the tomb, and all withdrew.*

Enter into that total emptiness and grief of each of those—Mary, Peter, the beloved disciple, Mary Magdalen—who loved Jesus so much.

It is this gaping emptiness that prepares them to receive the experience of the resurrection.

At some time during this week, perhaps on this day, pray over the reading for Good Friday, the great Song of the Suffering Servant: Isaiah 52:13 - 53:12.

# God Dies on the Cross

The title above is a very interesting theological statement! Jesus died. Jesus is God. Jesus who is God died. This legitimizes the statement: 'God died'. Obviously it cannot mean that Jesus died precisely in virtue of his divinity. There is nothing of Nietzsche's 'death of God' or the 1960s 'God is dead' debate about this statement. What we are interested in here is not so much a theological speculation, but the depth and power of the spirituality contained in the statement, 'God dies on the cross'. It is simply a true and powerful way of bringing home to us the reality of what happened on Calvary. That God *did* die is a mystery totally beyond comprehension. For those willing to enter into it through contemplation, it is a mystery full of depth and power.

The great Sequence of the Easter Sunday liturgy, *Victimae Paschali,* expresses the paradox: 'The lamb has redeemed the sheep. Christ the innocent one has reconciled sinners to the Father'. As St Paul puts it: *For our sake God made the sinless one into sin, so that in him we might become the goodness of God* (2 Corinthians 5:21). The same Paul hopes that the cross will not be for us a 'stumbling block' as it was for the Jews, nor 'fool-ishness', as it was for the Greeks, but the power and the wisdom of God (1 Corinthians 1). That power and wisdom are the resurrection. It is pre-cisely in response to the totality of the self-empty-ing of Calvary that the totality of glory is bestowed in the resurrection.

Perhaps we catch a glimpse of total self-empty-ing in D.H. Lawrence's poem, 'Phoenix':

*Are you willing to be sponged out, erased,*
    *cancelled, made nothing?*
*Are you willing to be made nothing?*
*dipped into oblivion?*
*If not, you will never really change.*
*The phoenix renews her youth*
*only when she is burnt, burnt alive, burnt*
    *down*
*to hot and flocculent ash.*
*Then the small stirring of a new small bub in*
    *the nest*
*with strands of down like floating ash*
*Shows that she is renewing her youth like*
    *the eagle,*
*Immortal bird.*

Not only did Jesus, who is God, die; he died a death that he 'fully accepted' (Eucharistic Prayer 2). Because he totally emptied himself, he died the kind of death that he did—naked, humiliated, de-serted, a failure, in agony. In so far as I unite myself to his self-emptying, I unite myself to this death, and so to the resurrection.

The gospel by definition is Good News. The cru-cifixion is being re-enacted in the lives of countless people at this very moment. This is the 'news' aspect. In my contemplation I am not just taking a trip back into history to conjure up images of Jesus. I am put in touch with the same Jesus in his members who suffer here and now. The compassion I pray for is not some kind of 'warm inner glow', but the power of love to enter into people's struggles against evil and injustice in the world of today.

The 'good' aspect of this part of the 'news' is only comprehensible by faith. There is no way of averting or lessening the evil and injustice of our world by constructing theories about them. What we can do by entering into the crucifixion of Jesus is to be empowered with all the energy of his Spirit to struggle against evil and injustice, and then, when we are overtaken by powerlessness (as we must inevitably be), we can accept the injustice in union with Christ. This ultimate acceptance 'overcomes' the evil and renders it salvific by opening us to the Father's gift of the resurrection.

## Week 5
# *He is Risen*

H aving followed Jesus all the way to his death, we now rejoice with his followers who experience his resurrection, and we pray that we may be filled with joy at the joy and glory that Jesus now has as Lord.

### Day 1: Jesus appears to Mary, his mother
This is the only example of a resurrection experience presented in detail by St Ignatius in his Spiritual Exercises. He notes that it is not scriptural, but is demanded by the inner logic of the situation.

Very many people who have associated themselves closely with Mary in standing with her by the cross find this contemplation most helpful.

For others it seems unnecessary, Mary's faith not seeming to need such confirmation.

We are free to approach it however we wish. It certainly remains true that in proportion to the greatness of Mary's grief she is filled with the greatest consolation possible at the resurrection.

### Day 2: Matthew 28:1-10
The four gospels give different accounts of what happened at the dawn of Easter day.

We go with the women who loved Jesus and wanted to give the last honor to his body. We enter the imagery of earthquake, angel, stone rolled back, Jesus' appearance being like lightning, his garments white as snow.

All this suggests great awe and mystery.

Listen to the words: *'He is not here; he has risen as he said'. 'Do not be afraid'. 'Return to Galilee* (each one's 'home' place) *and there you will see me.'*

## Day 3: Contemplation to attain divine live

This is a great, all-embracing contemplation that St Ignatius presents at the end of the Spiritual Exercises to sum up and gather together all that has gone before.

Essentially, it consists in being present to as many as possible of the manifestations of God's love in our lives and in our world, and making as whole-hearted a response as we can.

It is through the resurrection that God reveals himself in our world, so in this contemplation we are in touch with the presence of the risen Lord.

During each of these weeks we take up part of the contemplation. This week we simply recall all the gifts that God gives: the vast variety of creation, our own personal life, our faith, Baptism, the Eucharist, and so on.

In loving response, we offer ourselves to the Lord in the famous prayer of St Ignatius:

'Take, Lord, and receive all my liberty, my memory, my understanding and my entire will— all that I have and possess. You have given all to me. To you, Lord, I return it. All is yours; dispose of it wholly according to your will. Give me only your love and your grace; this is enough for me.'

Remember here that when I offer to the Lord, I am the one who receives. To surrender all my liberty does not involve slavery but receiving the 'glorious liberty of the children of God'. To give my understanding means to receive his Wisdom. But I must focus on making the effort needed to *give*.

**Days 4,5,6**
Return to *repetition*. Or read Acts 2:14-36 and Colossians 3:1-4 (the reading from the Mass of Easter Sunday).

# The Resurrection

I f *Christ is not risen, our preaching is in vain, and your faith also* (1 Corinthians 15:14). The resurrection is everything; without it there is nothing. *The Dogmatic Constitution on Divine Revelation* of Vatican II established the very important principle of the hierarchy of truths. In that hierarchy this one truth, that the Lord is risen, is pre-eminent. The resurrection has transformed the whole of creation. The words of the hymn 'All the earth proclaim the Lord' are literally fulfilled. Every activity in nature, every act of a human person, the whole of history and each single detail take on a new, deeper dimension because the Lord is risen.

During the remainder of this Retreat at Home

we contemplate this present reality—the life of the risen Lord. Through the contemplation we enter more deeply into what is in fact the here and now reality of our lives. Every breath we inhale is not just air; it is the life of the one who is Lord. In the words of St Ignatius, the grace we ask for in this contemplation is 'to be glad and rejoice intensely because of the great joy and glory of Christ, our Lord'.

This petition can be surprising in its altruism. As we become progressively more and more decentred from self through our contemplations, especially of the passion, we focus more and more on Jesus, 'the one whom my heart loves'. It is not surprising, then, that having stood by him in his ultimate failure on Calvary, we should want to congratulate him on his triumph.

I do not focus on 'what is in it for me', but on the Christ whom I love. As always, inevitably, I am the beneficiary. Not only that: I am empowered to be a better instrument for the coming of the Kingdom. The altruism involved in this prayer helps underline the fact that the joy of the resurrection is in no way superficial or easily attainable. Certainly it goes immeasurably beyond mere, natural optimism. It presupposes all the other graces of each of these Retreats at Home. It is proportional to the degree of my entering into the Lord's self-emptying and my sharing of the experience of Good Friday.

As we come to contemplate the resurrection, we find that the event itself cannot be captured by any of our human faculties. It is ultimate mystery. No video camera could have recorded the Lord's resurrection. Our imagination cannot put us in touch with this event. We can imagine a corpse revivifying, stirring, standing and beginning to move (as in the case of Lazarus), but the resurrection of Jesus is something different. All we can know about it is that one who died came alive with a new kind of existence—a truly human existence—in the flesh as well as in the spirit, but quite different from our earthly existence, and so escaping our human power to know.

The only way to 'know' what the resurrection is is to encounter the risen Lord. We encounter him in his Word, in Sacraments, in his people, especially in those who have already encountered him. Hence the supreme importance of witnesses. *'You will be my witnesses'* (Acts 1:8). *'The Lord has risen indeed, and has appeared to Simon'* (Luke 24:34. So we take up the Word and enter into the appearances of the risen Lord to those who had faith in him.

To be a Christian is essentially to live with the life of the risen Lord. This is the transformation brought about by our Baptism (Romans 6:3ff., Galatians 3:27). This does not mean that somehow there is a second kind of 'spiritual life' going on in parallel with our 'ordinary human life'. It means that our human life is, in reality, in its ordinariness far from ordinary! All that we do think, say, hope, long for is an expression of the Christ who lives in us. That life wells up and breaks forth in ways of which we are often unaware.

In this way each of us becomes a witness, and the Easter faith is re-kindled and passed on. In so far as we enter more fully into these contemplations, our Baptism and our witness grow stronger and stronger.

## Week 6
# *The Lord the Consoler*

J esus comes to those who loved him during his life-time and consoles them in their grief.

### Day 1: John 20:11-18
Mary Magdalen is a model of our spiritual life.

In her sin and degradation she met Jesus who brought her salvation and hope. She became a disciple and walked with him. She followed him all the way to the cross.

Now, out of her grief, she meets the Lord in a new way that can never be taken away. Yet she cannot remain in the experience of his presence; she must go on mission and live by faith.

I hear addressed to me the Lord's words to Mary. I hear him call me gently by my name.

*'Do not cling to me ... Go and tell the brothers.'* She must let go of this experience and go on mission.

### Day 2: John 20:19-23
Jesus comes to meet his friends precisely in their fear.

He brings his peace. He gives them his mission.

This contemplation can greatly enrich our sharing of the peace at the Eucharist.

### Day 3: John 20:24-29
Jesus meets each one according to his or her personality.

He responds to Thomas' brashness. It is precisely the doubt of Thomas that is transformed into the gospel's only profession that Jesus is God.

Can I allow myself to open up to the power of the risen Lord in those ways in which I need to be transformed? Jesus invites me, like Thomas, to use the powerful sense of touch to contemplate him in his risen life.

*'Put your finger into my hands; put your hand into my side.'*

### Day 4: Continue the contemplation to attain divine love.
Last week we looked over some of the countless great gifts that God gives. He gives not only the gifts, but *himself* in and with every gift.

I look at some of God's gifts to me, focusing on his self-giving in each one.

*'He is all things; he is in all things'* (Colossians 3:11).

I allow the Lord, who is giving himself so totally to me, to draw my affection, and, as I feel moved, respond with 'Take, Lord, and receive', the prayer of Ignatius (see pages 127-8).

While it is most appropriate for the affections to be drawn, we cannot, of course, predict this. It is most helpful to make the offering with or without feelings.

**Days 5 and 6**

I return in *repetition* to anything that moved me in the above contemplations. Or I take up the great chapter on the resurrection, 1 Corinthians 15, and pray verses 3-11 and verses 20-28.

# Resurrection Appearances

The gospel narratives after the resurrection stress the real, bodily nature of the Lord's new life, but at the same time, its radical difference from his pre-resurrection earthly life.

One of the most striking differences is that Jesus no longer 'lives among' people as before, but 'appears' mysteriously from time to time. There is no indication of where he is between apparitions. The apparitions are to 'certain chosen witnesses' (Acts 10:41). In most cases these witnesses are those who already had a long relationship with him—like Mary Magdalen, Peter, the beloved disciple—and who are now ready for the new faith-relationship that the resurrection brings. In other cases, classically that of Paul, Jesus breaks into a person's life in a dramatically new way.

The resurrection appearances of the gospels give us a model of how the Lord operates now, today, in people's lives. *Now* is the resurrection time.

One thing clear about the resurrection appearances is that they are unclear. They are shrouded in mystery. The events are confused, the gospel accounts conflicting and irreconcilable. There is a great sense of urgency, much hurrying and running, instructions to go quickly (Matthew 27:7) as befits the last times. There is the almost universal initial failure to recognize the Lord (Luke 24:16,37; John 20:14, 21:4; Acts 9:5) suggesting that resurrection faith is a matter of growing gradually. For Paul, the rest of his life after Damascus, both prayer and apostolate, becomes an endless quest to grow in knowledge of Christ risen (see Galatians 1:15; Philippians 3:10).

The reaction of people who meet the risen Lord is not 'all beer and skittles'. There is a great mixture of emotions and levels of response in the gospel accounts of the apparitions, as there is in the lives of Christians today. Jesus leads his followers to peace and joy, sometimes gradually, sometimes through a sudden transformation. The fruit of the Spirit is love, peace, joy, patience, kindness, goodness, gentleness, faithfulness, self-control (Galatians 5:22). But this fruit is quite compatible with the need to grow through a cluster of negative interior states.

The event of the resurrection leads to fear (Mark 16:5,8; Luke 24:5,37; John 20:19) and doubt (Mark 16:11; Matthew 28:17; Luke 24:38; John 20:25). Fear and joy are present simultaneously (Matthew 28:8). The disciples even 'disbelieve for joy' (Luke 24:41). The words of encouragement, *'Do not be afraid'*, need to be repeated (Mark 16:6; Matthew 25:8,10). Jesus comes to meet different persons according to their differing personalities, situations, needs. He responds to the doubts of Thomas (John 20), the denials of Peter (John 21), the despair of the Emmaus disciples (Luke 24), the grief of Magdalen (John 20).

There is the important symbolism of the return to Galilee. The disciples are instructed to go to their own place and there they will meet the risen Lord. It is even in returning to fishing that they meet him (John 21). Resurrection faith involves 'coming home to ourselves', accepting and embracing the whole of our personality and our life journey as being God's gift to us, even the parts we feel like rejecting—even the sin, which is now totally forgiven.

Others meet the Lord on a journey, in listening to the Scriptures, in the breaking of bread. The great Emmaus story emphasises that Jesus is eminently 'meetable' in the Liturgy. The Lord comes to people who are loving, grieving, searching, afraid, disbelieving, despairing, walking, running, fishing, gathered together, going off alone, in a locked room, by a lake, on a mountainside. We too meet the Lord in the ordinariness of our complex daily lives. Hence the link between the resurrection and the Contemplation to Attain Divine Love.

The encounter with the risen Lord brings about a change that is profound, on the level of union and mission, as in our Baptism. The denouement of Matthew's gospel points this up very well. When the disciples gather to meet Jesus on the mountain they worship him, though some doubt. He promises to be with them, not necessarily to remove all doubt, but always, in every circumstance, exterior and interior, to 'be with'. To worshippers and doubters alike he gives the great mission to all peoples.

## Week 7

# *The Breaking of Bread*

To each of us the Lord gives the opportunity to encounter him and to experience the power of his resurrection in his Word, in nature, in other persons, in all the creation, in the Sacraments, especially in the Eucharist.

The Emmaus story (Luke 24:13-35) ranks with the greatest of Luke's many outstanding, beautifully crafted stories. It also gives a profound insight into the life of the early Church, and how it was seen as a living of the life of the risen Jesus.

### Day 1: Verses 13-14
Enter into the profound disappointment of these two disciples.

They go away (see John 6:66-67). They leave the church community.

*'We had hoped'*—words of extraordinary poignancy. All is now lost, even hope itself.

They are in despair. The only faint glimmer of hope is in the fact that they do two things: they walk and they *talk*. They go over and over the events, telling their story about all that has happened.

I am invited always to be in dialogue about the stories of my life.

### Day 2: Verses 15-17

It is in the telling of the story that Jesus begins to walk with them.

They do not recognize him. The revelation will be gradual. They need to be gradually drawn from where they are. The Emmaus story provides a model of the early church's *catechesis*.

Jesus walks beside me every day, every step. I pray to recognize and share his presence more and more.

### Day 3: Verses 18-24

Jesus draws them out, to tell their story to him.

How does the risen Lord act powerfully in my life, bringing me to greater freedom?

The story is full of powerful phrases: *'the things that have happened in Jerusalem in these days'; 'a prophet mighty in word and deed'; 'how they crucified him'.*

*'Our own hope had been ...'*: these are words of ultimate despair.

*'To set Israel free'.* Ironically, this is what is now happening.

### Day 4: Verses 25-27

*'You foolish men.'* Foolish indeed! Despite the admitted testimony of the women and their friends, they do not believe.

Jesus breaks open the word of Scripture for them. We need to listen carefully really to hear the hard word about the necessity of suffering in order to enter into glory.

## Day 5: Verses 28-35

They press him to stay. *'Ask and you will receive.'*

As in the Eucharist, Jesus took bread, said the blessing, broke it and gave it to them. How much do I recognize him at the Eucharist?

He vanished. The experience may be fleeting, but the transformation is total. *'Were not our hearts burning?'* (I look into my own heart.) They return, and now tell the *full* story.

## Day 6: Contemplation to attain divine love.

The Lord not only gives gifts, and gives himself with and in them, but he is constantly at *work* to give me life and to unite me to myself. See Proverbs 8:22-36 and John 5:17.

I reflect on God's ceaseless activities on my behalf, and I respond with Ignatius' prayer: 'Take, Lord, and receive ...' (see pages 127-8).

# The Life of the Risen Lord

The constant refrain of Acts, the Epistles and the Book of Revelation is that the resurrection of Jesus Christ is the centre of all Christian life. Here are a few quotes that may encourage us to explore these writings further:

*Let the house of Israel know assuredly that God has made him both Lord and Christ, this Jesus whom you crucified* (Acts 2:36).

*He was designated Son of God in power according*

*to the Spirit of holiness by his resurrection from the dead* (Romans 1:3).

*At the name of Jesus every knee should bow and every tongue confess that Jesus Christ is Lord to the glory of God the Father* (Philippians 2:11).

*He is the beginning, the first-born from the dead, that in everything he might be pre-eminent* (Colossians 1:18).

*Christ is all things, and in all things* (Colossians 3:11).

*If Christ is not risen, our preaching is in vain, and your faith also* (1 Corinthians 15:14).

*But in fact Christ has been raised from the dead, the first fruits of those who have fallen asleep ... When all things are subjected to him, then the Son himself will also be subjected to him who put all things under him, that God may be all in all* (1 Corinthians 15:20-28).

*Blessed be the God and Father of our Lord Jesus Christ, who in raising Jesus Christ from the dead has given us new birth as his sons* (1 Peter 1:3).

*God, the giver of all grace, has called us to enjoy, after a little suffering, his eternal glory in Christ Jesus* (1 Peter 5:10).

*We were baptised into his death, so that as Christ was raised from the dead by the glory of the Father we too might live a new life* (Romans 6:4).

*You will be saved if you confess with your lips that Jesus is Lord, and believe in your heart that God raised him from the dead* (Romans 10:9).

*No one can say Jesus is Lord except by the Holy Spirit* (1 Corinthians 12:3).

*For me to live is Christ* (Philippians 1:21).

*I want to be found in him, not having a righteousness of my own based on law, but that which is through faith in Christ: that I may know him and the power of his resurrection* (Philippians 3:9-10).

*Since you have received Christ Jesus, the Lord, live your whole lives in him ... full of thanksgiving* (Colossians 2:6).

*For you have died, and your life is hidden with Christ in God. When Christ who is our life appears, you too will be revealed with him in all your glory* (Colossians 3:3-4).

*We believe that Jesus underwent death and rose again; just so, when Jesus comes back, God will bring back those who have found rest in him.* (1 Thessalonians 4:14).

*When the goodness and loving kindness of God our Saviour appeared, he saved us, not because of deeds done by us in righteousness, but in virtue of his own mercy, by the washing of regeneration and renewal in the Holy Spirit, which he poured out upon us richly through Jesus Christ our Saviour, so that we might be justified by his grace and become heirs to eternal life* (Titus 3:4-7).

*Go on singing and chanting to the Lord in your hearts, always and for everything giving thanks in the name of our Lord Jesus Christ to God the Father (Ephesians 5:19-20).*

*The kingdom of the world has become the kingdom*

*of our Lord and of his Christ, and he shall reign for ever and ever (Revelation 11:15).*

Week 8

# Do You Love Me?

The short series of post-resurrection appearances concludes, and Jesus commissions
his disciples to hand on the life of faith
right to the present day—till the end of time.

## Day 1: John 21:1-14
The disciples return to their Galilee homeland.
They return to their community, but are still 'at a
loose end'.

*Let's go fishing.'* It is in taking up their usual
occupation that they meet the Lord.

Enter into the scene: their straining to see the
mysterious figure through the mists on the shore.
They help one another to recognize the Lord.

He comes to them according to their different
personalities: to the clear-sighted 'beloved disciple', to Peter in his impetuous jumping overboard.
Admire the exquisite hospitality of the risen Lord
in barbecuing a fish for their breakfast. Fish, the
symbol of Christian salvation.

## Day 2: John 21:15-23
A scene of many facets.

The reparation of Peter's triple denial.

The commission to the new leader to exercise authority as shepherd.

A profound teaching on the nature of spiritual encounter with the risen Lord.

Peter is now very different, He is humble, having had the experience of humiliation. He ignores the Lord's 'bait', *'more than these others'*. His love depends not on his own power, but on the Lord's life-giving knowledge.

Yet he is the same—annoyed at being asked three times, inquisitive about the beloved disciple.

As a result of our making these three Retreats at Home, we remain the same person with the same personality, but with a radically new relationship.

## Day 3: Matthew 28:16-20

The great mission given to all—a mixture of worshipers and doubters.

'Baptize them *into* the name (i.e. life) of Father, Son and Holy Spirit'—a quotation of the liturgical formula of the early Church. The grace I have received and must hand on.

'I am *with* you.' The theme of Matthew's gospel. See Matthew 1:23.

The Lord is with us in all things—not solving our problems, but present in all of them.

## Day 4: Contemplation to attain divine love

I look again at some of the myriad gifts of God to me, and consider how every one of them is a pale reflection of his infinite beauty, goodness, love and compassion. I praise him, perhaps using Psalms 145-150, and I respond, as always, with 'Take, Lord, and receive' (pages 127-8).

### Day 5: Luke 24:50-53 and Acts 1:6-14

Luke's pictorial presentation of the 'departure' of Jesus as an ascension.

I return with the disciples to the upper room in union with Mary to pray and to wait ...

### Day 6:

Take up *repetition* of any of the previous days' prayer.

# Awareness Examen

As a result of his resurrection, Christ is *all things and in all things* (Colossians 3:11). In the light of this truth, we seek awareness of our relationship with the Lord. Christ is our life (see Colossians 3:4). This is the reality. The trick is to be aware of it, to be in touch with the presence of the Lord in all things. The word 'things' has the broadest possible scope. It means not only objects or creatures, but very especially the most important class of creatures, persons. It means events, both external and internal (the inner experience of each person). For Ignatius of Loyola, the fruit of making his Spiritual Exercises, as we have done over these twenty-four weeks, was to be a growing facility in 'finding God in all things'.

The 'awareness examen' can be a most powerful instrument to put us more in touch with the presence of the Lord in every detail and aspect of our lives. It is recommended as the prayer to end each day, and also as a means of periodic review of our lives.

The exercise of the awareness examen has five stages:

1. We commence with the most basic of all prayers, gratitude. *In everything give thanks* (1 Thessalonians 5:18).

2. What is the *grace* I want? I want to be *aware,* not through a cerebral exercise, but by the light of the Holy Spirit; so I pray to God's Spirit to be with me, enlightening me and bringing me to awareness.

3. I begin to reflect and remember, to examine my thoughts and feelings, to become more aware of the Lord. He is the Creator and giver of all. He gives himself with and in every 'thing'. He is at work ceaselessly in his creation to lead us to himself. Every aspect of creation reflects the divine beauty, love and goodness.

I reflect on my experience today of:

(a) Nature: air, water, sun, rain, clouds, stars, bird life, animal life.

(b) Gifts made by human hand: buildings, bridges, electricity, the media, transport, communications.

(c) Persons: those I met today, those closest to me; the stranger; the underprivileged; the handicapped; those with whom I exchanged a smile, a word (unexpectedly?), my experience of respect or an act of kindness.

(d) Myself: my talents. Am I growing in awareness of God's gifts? My senses. How did I use each of these five today? My prayer. How was I aware of the Lord? My capacity to love. How was it engaged today? How was I challenged today? (e) Events: 'world events', the news. How do I relate these to the Kingdom of God? What evoked my wonder, concern, gratitude, anger, fear? The events of my world of work, play, relationships. (f) Inner events: my feelings today. Positive feelings towards God: gratitude, trust, response; positive feelings towards others. Negative feelings: anger, anxiety, lust, jealousy, etc.

How am I now called to find the Lord in these 'things'?

4. If I have become aware of any lack of love in my life today, I come before the Lord on the cross and I express my sorrow to him.

5. I look at the probable shape of my day tomorrow. I get in touch with the great gift of Christian hope, I ask the Lord's help, focusing especially on any planned meeting with another person or other planned event that will be of significance.

*Note*: In the above 'examination' (point no. 3), a person would never work through all the suggested points in one 'awareness examen' but would use different ones at different times.

Biblical Theol & Sys Ex
Weeds among the Wheat
God of Surprises /Gerald Hughes
Finding God in all things - Barry
Sadhana

Resp to 101 Q abt Jesus.
meet Jesus again for the 1st time.

_[number includes cover sheet]

ages of this document were not transmitted.

**SUIT RETREAT HOUSE**
**BOX 185**
**RADO   80135-0185**

303-688-9633